D0440582

THE PROSE EDDA

THE PROSE EDDA

OF SNORRI STURLUSON

TALES FROM

NORSE MYTHOLOGY

INTRODUCED BY

SIGURÐUR NORDAL, D.LITT. OXON.

*Research Professor of Icelandic Literature
in the University of Reykjavik*

SELECTED AND TRANSLATED BY

JEAN I. YOUNG

M.A., PH.D. CANTAB.

Senior Lecturer in English at the University of Reading

UNIVERSITY OF CALIFORNIA PRESS

BERKELEY, LOS ANGELES, LONDON

University of California Press
Berkeley and Los Angeles, California

University of California Press, Ltd.
London, England

First published in 1954 by
Bowes & Bowes Publishers Limited
Cambridge, England

Manufactured in the United States of America

ISBN 0-520-01232-1

17   18   19   20

CONTENTS

INTRODUCTION

One of the three most important manuscripts of Snorri's *Edda,*
the *Uppsala Codex* (a parchment from about 1320) is prefaced by
this statement: 'This book is called *Edda*; Snorri Sturluson wrote
it in the same order in which it is set out here. The first part is
about the Æsir and Ymir, then comes the *Skáldskaparmál* ('Poetic
Diction') and the names given to various things, last the *Háttatal*
('Account of Metres') which Snorri composed about King Hákon
and Duke Skúli.'

The whole of the first part 'about the Æsir and Ymir' — that is
Gylfaginning ('The Deluding of Gylfi') and the *Prologue* — is
included in the present translation. The second part consists in
the main of a catalogue of kennings (figurative expressions of
various kinds) whose use in ancient poetry is illustrated by
numerous examples. In the original this section is about the same
length as the first, but only the longer mythological and heroic
stories with which it is interspersed have been translated here.
The third part consists of the poem Snorri composed about King
Hákon and Earl (later Duke) Skúli Barðarson, between 1221 and
1223. This comprises 102 stanzas and the text is accompanied by
a commentary, in prose, on the variations of metre and style
exemplified by each verse. The whole of this section has been
omitted, since it would be impossible to translate a composition
of this kind into any other language.

Other early sources, besides the *Uppsala Codex,* establish

7

beyond dispute that only this work of Snorri Sturluson's has the right to the name of *Edda*. It is merely owing to a seventeenth-century misunderstanding that the poems, which it has since been the custom to call Eddic, were labelled *The Elder Edda* or *Sæmund's Edda*.

What does *Edda* mean? Opinions differ greatly. The most usual one is that the word is related to *óðr* ('poem, poetry') and may be translated 'Poetics', the book constituting a sort of *ars poetica*. Be this as it may, the second and third sections of the book undoubtedly form a guide to the use of early skaldic diction (skaldic verse was the usual medium of the Viking poets) and to the great diversity of metre and style exhibited by poetry in general. How then did the first part of the book take the form of a survey of ancient northern mythology, and what is the connection between it and the subsequent sections?

⊷ II ⊷

It is a matter of common knowledge that the richest and purest source extant for the ideas and attitude to life of the early Germanic peoples is the literature of Iceland during the twelfth and thirteenth centuries. This ancient inheritance is usually regarded as having been slowly destroyed by the impact of Christianity and other foreign influences during the period between the conversion of Iceland (in 1000) and about 1400. This is true enough as far as its beginning and end are concerned, but is far from being the whole story of Old Icelandic literature. Attack and resistance alternate. The literature of thirteenth-century Iceland is much more Icelandic than that of the twelfth, and when Snorri Sturluson's work is considered — and he played the greatest part in this change — it becomes clear that it is not only a question of defence but also of counter-attack.

This is most evident from Snorri's historical works.[1] Neither of the first Icelandic historians, the learned chieftains Sæmund Sigfússon (who died in 1133) and the more important Ári Thorgilsson (who died in 1148 — he founded a school that used the vernacular), wrote sagas. The writers of this school record dry, accurate information concerning the settlement, history of the commonwealth, ecclesiastical history, chronology, and so forth. Their writings are to the sagas what the earliest Greek annalists are to Herodotus. When the Icelanders began, after 1170, to write sagas about the events of bygone days (as well as about contemporary affairs, as, for example, in *Sverrir's Saga*), it was the monks who led the way and their heroes are the missionary kings of Norway, Ólaf Tryggvason and Saint Ólaf. When the sagas of these two kings, written and rewritten by various authors between 1180 and 1220, are compared with those Snorri wrote about them, we are apt to think only of a literary development, as Snorri's sagas are both more realistic and more entertaining. Snorri's ruthless handling of these earlier sagas, his sources, is, however, not due solely to his greater critical acumen and stricter regard for truth. Rationalistic layman and chieftain as he was, he was repelled by the ecclesiastical spirit pervading the sagas in question — all the way from the legendary tales, sermons of edification, pious remarks and unctuous style, to the very delineation of character and interpretation of events themselves. In fact, behind all this is the political struggle between the old families of the aristocracy, who from the period of the conversion of Iceland had exercised complete authority over the church, and the bishops of the twelfth century and later, who were endeavouring to make the church as independent and powerful as it was in the rest of Europe — a state within the state.

---

1 *Saint Ólaf's Saga* and *Heimskringla* ('Orb of the World'). Snorri also wrote *Egil's Saga*. He is thus the author of four of the most famous books in Icelandic.

If we bear in mind that Snorri's historical work shows this tendency we shall, I think, get closer to understanding the place in the literature and culture of Iceland occupied by his *Edda*. It is something different from, and more than, a 'text-book of poetics', a collection of rules which poets of earlier days had learned by word of mouth from their predecessors and passed on from one generation to another. This seems quite clear from the conclusion of the first chapter of *Poetic Diction* where Snorri is speaking in his own person: 'Now to young poets who want to study poetic diction and enrich their style with ancient designations or who wish to understand the hidden meaning of poetry, I would say, let them peruse this book to their profit and pleasure. Neglect and distrust these stories as we may, we should not go so far as to remove from poetry ancient kennings which the great poets of old permitted themselves to enjoy. Christians, however, must not believe in pagan gods or that these tales are true in any other way than is indicated at the beginning of this book.' It is evident that these words refer to a dispute and it is easy to recognize the fanatics against whom they are directed.

During Snorri's lifetime (1179-1241) the ancient art of Icelandic poetry was threatened on two sides. In the first place a narrow-minded clergy, in their desire to obliterate every trace of heathenism, had gone so far as to banish the names of the old gods from those of the days of the week (in Icelandic, Tuesday, Wednesday, Thursday and Friday are called Third Day, Midweek-day, Fifth Day and Fast Day respectively). It was no wonder that they considered it sinful for poetry to incorporate all the ancient mythological kennings which were incomprehensible without some knowledge of the myths of the Æsir. At the same time, during the twelfth century a new fashion in poetry had been introduced into Iceland which had become very popular with the common people — the *dance*. This was an improvisation of four lines whose everyday words were set to a loose rhythm in which even the most elementary of the old metrical rules were disregarded. Snorri, in his account of the kennings in *Poetic Diction*, carefully specifies, amongst other things, the way in which all the ancient gods are to be designated and, in his *Account of Metres* and the explanations of these given in that work, he begins with the difficult Court Metre (*dróttkvætt*) which he regards as the most refined of them all and lays down the most meticulous rules for the correct use of alliteration. In this way he tells his 'young poets' all that he considers it most important for them to learn and pass on. They are not to be so narrow-minded or timid as to avoid the kennings found in mythology or they will cease to understand anything of the older poetry. Neither are they to practise their art in so commonplace and complacent a manner as to deprive themselves of all the magnificent and cunningly wrought diversity of poetic style and metre to be found in the work of the great poets of old.

⤙ I V ⤚

Why did Snorri, not content with writing the last two sections of the *Edda*, add to these the *Deluding of Gylfi* and its *Prologue* which are only remotely connected with a system of poetics? The answer is given in the words quoted above: 'Christians, however, must not believe in pagan gods or that these tales are true in any other way than is indicated at the beginning of this book.' It was a customary belief in the Middle Ages, evident from the legendary sagas of the kings of Norway previously mentioned, that the ancient gods, particularly Thór and Óðin, did really exist: that they were devils and evil spirits that might appear in many shapes to tempt men and do them various injuries. By denouncing these superstitions Snorri, at one and the same time, administered a rebuke to the clergy, whilst safeguarding himself from any attack on the grounds that he was preaching heathenism to young poets. Consider the *Prologue* and stories that form the framework for the *Deluding of Gylfi*. In the first chapter of the *Prologue*, which apparently consists of Snorri's own reflections, since no model or source for them has been found, either foreign or Icelandic, he tries to show that there is a natural and common basis for all forms of religion and to explain how they have branched out from this stock. He then turns to the widely held euhemeristic theory that the Æsir had been kings and chieftains who, by men of a later period, had come to be looked on as gods. Even this does not satisfy him, however. By making the 'Men of Asia' themselves work magic for Gylfi and relate to him the stories of the gods in order to tempt him to believe in them (see the last chapter of the *Deluding of Gylfi*) Snorri has finally ensured himself complete liberty to say all he wants. He can now tell the 'Saga' of the world and the gods all the way from Ymir to Ragnarök, interspersing it with his own reflections (concerning, for example, the origin of life) and setting it forth in all its splendour and power, its comic and its tragic aspects. And while the scholar and poet in him are relating this instructive and entertaining tale, it is as if he were glancing over his shoulder at the clergy and asking, 'What reason can there be for hating and despising a faith which, after all, served our forefathers as a guide to a life of courage and achievement?'

―← V →―

We know now that in some respects Snorri's mythology is not in full agreement with the ancient mythological poems which to a great extent constitute his sources, and that neither it, nor they, give us an idea of Scandinavian heathenism as it really was. Much of the mythology and many of the stories about the gods are simply the product of the poetic imagination and derive from speculation current during the decline of paganism, occasionally mingled with ideas and motifs that are Christian and southern in origin.

No one now reads the *Deluding of Gylfi* as a text-book on mythology but, whereas under the impact of fresh research all more recent text-books have become and will continue to become antiquated, not one of them can make the *Deluding of Gylfi* out of date. This is so partly because in it Snorri relates various stories found nowhere else, but first and foremost because it is a work of art and its stories will never be told better.

It must be admitted that Snorri's *Edda* makes an appeal to the modern reader mainly because the author, in relating the *Deluding of Gylfi*, forgot the chief purpose of his book and, in his account of their doings and destiny, brought the gods to life again entirely for their own sakes. It is, nevertheless, natural to ask what, in view of this purpose, was the influence of the book on contemporary and later times?

In our own time it is a matter of general experience and, perhaps, of still more general belief that it is not only difficult but futile to resist 'progress' and try to put the clock back. We know, however, that the preservation of old values is an indispensable counterpart to the creation of new. The influence exerted by Snorri Sturluson is a good example of the way in which these two things may go hand in hand.

Snorri himself preserved in his writings almost all the best ninth- and tenth-century skaldic poetry, both Norwegian and Icelandic, still extant. There is also good reason to believe that it is owing to his *Edda* that the poems we now know as *The Elder Edda* were collected and set down in writing. The impulse he gave kindled a new attitude to and fresh understanding of pagan culture and philosophy of life, which is reflected in those sagas of past times that were written after his day. It is largely owing to him that, as W. P. Ker says, 'the heroic age of the ancient Germans may be said to culminate, and end, in Iceland in the thirteenth century'.

What about the art of poetry itself? There is no doubt that the tripping lyrical *dances* went on being made up after Snorri's time, but they were held in such low esteem compared with 'refined' poetry that, it may be said, unfortunately, hardly any survive. On the other hand, the old form of poetic composition enjoyed a sort of renaissance in the poems of Snorri's two nephews who clearly followed his lead. These were Ólaf Thórðarson *hvítaskáld* (White Poet, died 1259) and Sturla Thórðarson (died 1282). Moreover, although round about 1300 Icelanders ceased to be employed as court poets by foreign rulers, Court Metre containing fewer kennings but exhibiting otherwise traditional rhythms and style went on being used for religious verse and, in this form, reached its high point in *Lilja* ('The Lily') in the middle of the fourteenth century. The ancient art won its greatest victory, however, when the Icelanders created — from grafting the heroic ballad (the form of poetry most typical of thirteenth- to fifteenth-century Scandinavia) with certain characteristics of the older kind of verse — a new branch of poetry, the *rímur* ('rhyming lays'). In the *rímur* not only are all the rules governing alliterative verse strictly kept, as is still the case in all Icelandic poetry, but they themselves are composed in exact conformity with Snorri's demands: that is, they exhibit great diversity of splendid metres and use of kennings, in particular heathen kennings. It is noteworthy, too, that their authors constantly employ expressions like 'Eddic rule, Eddic art'. *Rímur* began to be composed in Iceland soon after 1350 and have enjoyed a remarkable popularity in that they were still being composed in a similar style down to our own time. Further, metrically and stylistically they have exerted a strong direct and indirect influence on the rest of Icelandic poetry. Although the *rímur* poets, like the poets before the days of Snorri, could have learned their art from their predecessors and from older poems, it has long been the custom for them to study the *Edda* both in order 'to enrich their style' and 'to understand the hidden meaning of poetry'. When trends in modern poetry are discussed in Iceland today, even if traditionalists do not quote Snorri in quite the same way as the younger poets quote T. S. Eliot and Paul Eluard, he looms up, nevertheless, behind certain of their ideas. And whatever we may think of the poetical value of the *rímur* and other verse in the old tradition, there is no question of the important consequences of the general devotion to this kind of poetry — the most obvious of these, perhaps, being the preservation of the classical language of the thirteenth century as the living Icelandic of today.

SIGURÐUR NORDAL

TRANSLATOR'S FOREWORD

Snorri Sturluson (1179-1241) was a man of many talents. Astute at business and a diplomat, highly educated and travelled, he early acquired great wealth and power, twice occupying the highest office in Iceland and being singled out for special honour by a foreign potentate. Yet, able as he was in practical affairs, his chief interest in life was in literature. Iceland's most famous man of letters, he wrote four major works of very different character. Two were biographies — *St. Ólaf's Saga* and *Egil's Saga*, the one about the great eleventh-century king who became Norway's patron saint, the other about the famous Icelandic Viking poet who once fought as a mercenary in this country during the wars of the tenth century. *Heimskringla* records the lives of the kings of Norway from the early sixth to the late twelfth century. *The Prose Edda*, with which this translation is concerned, was intended as a handbook for poets who, in Snorri's day, were forgetting how to compose in the 'high style' of their predecessors, the skalds or court poets of the Viking Age. The titles of the second and third sections of this work, *Skáldskaparmál* and *Háttatal* (*Poetic Diction* and *Account of Metres*), indicate their content. The first section, however, *Gylfaginning* (*The Deluding of Gylfi*), couched in the form of a conversation between a prehistoric Swedish King Gylfi and three knowledgeable beings known as High, Just-as-High, and Third, is in reality a sophisticated guide to Northern mythology based on poems, some of which are looked on as older than any skaldic verse. By virtue of its author's sympathy and humour, irony and detachment, *The Deluding of Gylfi* is one of the great story-books of the Middle Ages.

The last translation into English of *The Prose Edda*, that of the American scholar, A. G. Brodeur, was made almost forty years ago. It was published in 1916 and has been reprinted three times since. The time, therefore, seems ripe for a new translation which will make available in more modern idiom Snorri's inimitable stories about the gods and heroes of the Northern peoples. In undertaking this translation I have had in mind two kinds of persons — the university student and the general reader. To meet the needs of the student I have aimed at a faithful rendering of my author's meaning, although I hope that I have also achieved an interpretation that will not strike the general reader as pedantic. I had this reader in mind when selecting my material. People remember *The Heroes of Asgard* with affection, and the fact that *Myths of the Norseman* has been reprinted many times between 1908 and 1948 indicates that there is a public outside university circles that is perennially interested in Northern story-telling. The present translation, therefore, consists of narrative portions of *The Prose Edda*: it includes the whole of *The Deluding of Gylfi* and all the longer heroic tales incorporated in *Poetic Diction*. What the rest of Snorri's *Edda* is about, why he wrote it and its fundamental importance for Icelandic literature will be gathered from the *Introduction* by Sigurður Nordal, the scholar, to whom more than to anyone else the student of Snorri is indebted today.

The Icelandic text used for this translation is that of the Norwegian, Anne Holtsmark, and the Icelander, Jón Helgason, professors of Northern Languages and Literature in the Universities of Oslo and Copenhagen respectively. Published in Copenhagen in 1950, it was the most recent available when this translation was made. I have also consulted the complete edition of *The Prose Edda* by Finnur Jónsson, revised in 1926, and the Arnamagnæan edition of 1848-87.

The spellings of Icelandic names in a translation of this kind presents certain difficulties. Many of these names exhibit initial and final combinations of consonants with which the general reader may be unfamiliar — for example Hlín, Baldr. Since, however, many people prefer a foreign work to have a foreign flavour and there is, moreover, a general tendency amongst scholars in this country today to keep foreign words as far as possible in their native forms, this is the course adopted here, thus even Thór, Óðin, etc.[1] Valhalla is one of the exceptions.

I should like first and foremost to thank Sigurður Nordal, now Icelandic Minister in Copenhagen, for his masterly *Introduction*, and to acknowledge the kind help and encouragement of Professor Bruce Dickins, Elrington and Bosworth Professor of Anglo-Saxon in the University of Cambridge. I owe much, too, to my father, the late J. T. Young. To the University of Reading I am indebted for a grant towards expenses of publication.

---

[1] It will be noticed, however, that inflexional *-r*, *-l*, *-n* are dropped. The symbol ð is used for the corresponding Icelandic ð and Th for the initial þ.

PROLOGUE

AND

THE DELUDING
OF GYLFI

PROLOGUE

In the beginning Almighty God created heaven and earth and
everything that goes with them and, last of all, two human
beings, Adam and Eve, from whom have come families. Their
progeny multiplied and spread over all the world. As time went
on, however, inequalities sprang up amongst peoples — some
were good and righteous but by far the greater number, dis-
regarding God's commandments, turned to the lusts of the world.
For this reason God drowned the world and all creatures living
in it — with the exception of those who were with Noah in the
ark. Eight persons survived Noah's flood and these peopled the
world and founded families. As the population of the world
increased, however, and a larger area became inhabited, the same
thing happened again; the great majority of mankind, loving the
pursuit of money and power, left off paying homage to God.
This grew to such a pitch that they boycotted any reference to
God, and then how could anyone tell their sons about the marvels
connected with Him? In the end they lost the very name of God
and there was not to be found in all the world a man who knew
his Maker. Notwithstanding, God granted them earthly gifts,
worldly wealth and prosperity, and He also bestowed on them
wisdom so that they understood all earthly things and all the
ways in which earth and sky were different from each other.
They observed that in many respects the earth and birds and
beasts have the same nature and yet exhibit different behaviour,

and they wondered what this signified. For instance, one could dig down into the earth on a mountain peak no deeper than one would in a low-lying valley and yet strike water; in the same way, in both birds and beasts, the blood lies as near to the surface of the skin of the head as of the foot. Another characteristic of the earth is that every year grass and flowers grow on it and that same year wither and die; similarly fur and feathers grow and die every year on beasts and birds. There is a third thing about the earth: when its surface is broken into and dug up, grass grows on the topsoil. Mountains and boulders they associated with the teeth and bones of living creatures, and so they looked on earth as in some way a living being with a life of its own. They knew it was inconceivably ancient as years go, and by nature, powerful; it gave birth to all things and owned all that died, and for that reason they gave it a name and reckoned their descent from it. They also learned from their ancestors that the same earth and sun and stars had been in existence for many centuries, but that the procession of the stars was unequal; some had a long journey, others a short one. From things like this they guessed that there must be someone who ruled the stars, who, if he desired, could put an end to their procession, and that he must be very powerful and strong. They reckoned too, that, if he controlled the primal elements, he must have existed before the heavenly bodies; and they realized that, if he guided these, he must rule over the shining of the sun and the dew-fall and the growth of plants resultant on these, and the winds of the air and storms of the sea as well. They did not know where his kingdom was, but they believed that he ruled everything on earth and in the sky, heaven and the stars, the ocean and all weathers. In order that this might be related and kept in mind, they gave their own names to everything, but with the migrations of peoples and multiplication of languages this belief has changed in many ways. They understood everything in a material sense, however, since they had not been given spiritual understanding, and so they thought that everything had been made from some substance.

The world was divided into three parts. From south to west up to the Mediterranean was the part known as Africa, and the southern portion of this is so hot that everything there is burned by the sun. The second part, running from west to north up to the ocean, is called Europe or Énéa, and the northern half of this is so cold that no grass grows there and it is uninhabited. From north to east and down to the south is Asia, and these regions of the world have great beauty and magnificence; the earth yields special products like gold and precious stones. The centre of the world is there also, and just as the earth there is more fertile and in every way superior to that found elsewhere, so the human beings living there were endowed beyond their fellows with all manner of gifts — wisdom, strength, beauty and every kind of ability.

Near the centre of the world where what we call Turkey lies, was built the most famous of all palaces and halls — Troy by name. That town was built on a much larger scale than others then in existence and in many ways with greater skill, so lavishly was it equipped. There were twelve kingdoms with one over-king, and each kingdom contained many peoples. In the citadel were twelve chieftains and these excelled other men then living in every human fashion. One of the kings was called Múnón or Mennón. He married a daughter of the chief king Priam who was called Tróán, and they had a son named Trór — we call him Thór. He was brought up in Thrace by a duke called Loricus and, when he was ten years old, he received his father's arms. When he took his place amongst other men he was as beautiful to look at as ivory inlaid in oak; his hair was lovelier than gold. At twelve years old he had come to his full strength and then he lifted ten bear pelts from the ground at once and killed his foster-father Loricus with his wife Lóri or Glóri, and took possession of the realm of Thrace — we call that Thrúðheim. After that he travelled far and wide exploring all the regions of the world and by himself overcoming all the berserks and giants and an enormous dragon and many wild beasts. In the northern part of the world he met with and married a prophetess called Sibyl whom we call Sif. I do not know Sif's genealogy but she was a most beautiful woman with hair like gold. Lóriði, who resembled his father, was their son. Lóriði's son was Einridi, his son Vingethór, his son Vingener, his son Módi, his son Magi, his son Seskef, his son Beðvig, his son Athra, whom we call Annar, his son Ítrmann, his son Heremóð, his son Skjaldun, whom we call Skjöld, his son Bíaf whom we call Bjár, his son Ját, his son Guðólf, his son Finn, his son Fríallaf whom we call Friðleif; he had a son named Vóden whom we call Óðin; he was a man famed for his wisdom and every kind of accomplishment. His wife was called Frígíða, whom we call Frigg.

Óðin, and also his wife, had the gift of prophecy, and by means of this magic art he discovered that his name would be famous in the northern part of the world and honoured above that of all kings. For this reason he decided to set out on a journey from Turkey. He was accompanied by a great host of old and young, men and women, and they had with them many valuables. Through whatever lands they went such glorious exploits were related of them that they were looked on as gods rather than men. They did not halt on their journey until they came to the north of the country now called Germany. There Óðin lived for a long time taking possession of much of the land and appointing three of his sons to defend it. One was called Vegdeg; he was a powerful king and ruled over East Germany; his son was Vitrgils; his sons were Vitta, father of Heingest, and Sigar, father of Svebdag, whom we call Svipdag. Óðin's second son was called Beldeg, whom we call Baldr; he had the country now called Westphalia; his son was Brand; his son, Frjóðigar, whom we call Fróði; his son, Freóvin; his son, Wigg; his son, Gevis, whom we call Gave. Óðin's third son was called Sigi; his son, Rerir; this pair ruled over what is now called France, and the family known as Völsungar come from there. Great and numerous kindreds have come from all of them. Then Óðin set off on his journey north and coming to the land called Reiðgotaland took possession of everything he wanted in that country. He appointed his son Skjöld to govern there; his son was Friðleif; from thence has come the family known as Skjöldungar; they are kings of Denmark and what was then called Reiðgotaland is now named Jutland.

Thereafter Óðin went north to what is now called Sweden. There was a king there called Gylfi and, when he heard of the expedition of the men of Asia, as the Æsir were called, he went to meet them and offered Óðin as much authority over his kingdom as he himself desired. Their travels were attended by such prosperity that, wherever they stayed in a country, that region enjoyed good harvests and peace, and everyone believed that they caused this, since the native inhabitants had never seen any other people like them for good looks and intelligence. The plains and natural resources of life in Sweden struck Óðin as being favourable and he chose there for himself a town-site now called Sigtuna. There he appointed chieftains after the pattern of Troy, establishing twelve rulers to administer the laws of the land, and he drew up a code of law like that which had held in Troy and to which the Trojans had been accustomed. After that, he travelled north until he reached the sea, which they thought encircled the whole world, and placed his son over the kingdom now called Norway. Their son was called Sæming and, as it says in the *Háleygjatal*,[1] together with the earls and other rulers the kings of Norway trace their genealogies back to him. Óðin kept by him the son called Yngvi, who was king of Sweden after him, and from him have come the families known as Ynglingar. The Æsir and some of their sons married with the women of the lands they settled, and their families became so numerous in Germany and thence over the north that their language, that of the men of

1 The 'Helgeland Genealogies'.

Asia, became the language proper to all these countries. From the fact that their genealogies are written down, men suppose that these names came along with this language, and that it was brought here to the north of the world, to Norway, Sweden, Denmark and Germany, by the Æsir. In England, however, there are ancient district and place names which must be understood as deriving from a different language.

THE DELUDING
OF GYLFI

King Gylfi ruled the lands that are now called Sweden. It is told
of him that he gave a ploughland in his kingdom, the size four
oxen could plough in a day and a night, to a beggar-woman as a
reward for the way she had entertained him. This woman, however, was of the family of the Æsir; her name was Gefjon. From
the north of Giantland she took four oxen and yoked them to a
plough, but those were her sons by a giant. The plough went in
so hard and deep that it loosened the land and the oxen dragged
it westwards into the sea, stopping in a certain sound. There
Gefjon set the land for good and gave it a name, calling it Zealand.
But the place where the land had been torn up was afterwards a
lake. It is now known in Sweden as 'The Lake'.[1] And there are as
many bays in 'The Lake' as there are headlands in Zealand. As the
poet Bragi the Old says:

> Gefjon dragged with laughter
> from Gylfi liberal prince
> what made Denmark larger,
> so that beasts of draught
> the oxen reeked with sweat;
> four heads they had, eight eyes to boot
> who went before broad island-pasture
> ripped away as loot.

King Gylfi was a wise man and skilled in magic. He marvelled
that the Æsir were so knowledgeable that everything came to

1 Mälar.

pass by their will, and he wondered if that was on account of their own strength or whether the divinities they worshipped brought that about. He set out on a secret journey to Ásgarð, changing himself into the likeness of an old man by way of disguise. But the Æsir were wiser than he, in that they had foreknowledge. They saw his journey before he came, and worked spells against him. When he came into the stronghold, he saw a hall so lofty that he could scarcely see over it; its roofing was covered with golden shields like a shingled roof. So Thjóðólf of Hvin says that Valhalla was roofed with shields:

> Fighting men showed prudence
> when with stones being pelted;
> they let the War-God's[1] roofing
> glitter on their backs.

Gylfi saw a man in the doorway who was juggling with knives, of which he had seven in the air at a time. This man at once asked him his name. He said he was called Gangleri and that he had come a long way, and he requested a lodging for himself for the night, asking who owned the hall. The other replied that it was their king. 'I can take you to see him, but you must ask him his name yourself'; and he wheeled round into the hall. Gylfi went after him, and at once the door shut on his heels. There he saw many rooms and a great number of people, some playing, others drinking, some had weapons and were fighting. As he looked about him much of what he saw puzzled him, and he said:

> At every door
> before you enter
> look around with care;
> you never know
> what enemies
> aren't waiting for you there.

He saw three high-seats one above the other, and a man seated in each of them. Then he asked what names those chieftains had. The man who had taken him inside answered that the one sitting

1 Sváfnir's, i.e. Óðin's.

on the lowest seat was a king called High One, the next was Just-as-high, and the topmost one was called Third. Then High One asked the stranger if he had any more business, although he was as welcome to food and drink as anyone else in High-hall. [Gylfi] replied that first of all he wanted to know if there was anyone within who was a well-informed man. High One said that he would not get out safe and sound unless he was still better informed:

> Whilst you ask, stand forward please,
> the answerer shall sit at ease.

Gylfi began his questioning: 'Who is the foremost or oldest of all the gods?'

High One replied: 'He is called All-father in our tongue, but in ancient Ásgarð he had twelve names: one is All-father; the second, Herran or Herjan;[1] the third, Nikar or Hnikar;[2] the fourth, Nikuz or Hnikuð;[3] the fifth, Fjölnir;[4] the sixth, Óski;[5] the seventh, Ómi;[6] the eighth, Bifliði or Biflindi;[7] the ninth, Sviðar; the tenth, Sviðrir; the eleventh, Viðrir;[8] the twelfth, Jálg or Jálk.'[9]

Then Gangleri asked: 'Where is that god? What power has he? What great deeds has he done?'

High One said: 'He lives for ever and ever, and rules over the whole of his kingdom and governs all things great and small.'

Then Just-as-high said: 'He created heaven and earth and the sky and all that in them is.'

Then Third said: 'His greatest achievement, however, is the making of man and giving him a soul which will live and never die, although his body may decay to dust or burn to ashes. All righteous men shall live and be with him where it is called Gimlé[10] or Vingólf,[11] but wicked men will go to Hel and thence to Niflhel[12] that is down in the ninth world.'

Then Gangleri said: 'What was he doing before heaven and earth were made?'

1 Lord or Raider.	5 Fulfiller-of-desire.	9 Gelding.
2 [Spear-]thruster.	6 One-whose-speech-resounds.	10 Lee-of-fire.
3 [Spear-]thruster.	7 Spear-shaker.	11 Friendly-floor.
4 Much-knowing.	8 Ruler-of-weather.	12 Abode-of-darkness.

High One replied: 'At that time he was with the frost ogres.'

Gangleri said: 'What was the origin of all things? How did they begin? What existed before?'

High One answered: 'As it says in the *Sibyl's Vision*:

> In the beginning
> not anything existed,
> there was no sand nor sea
> nor cooling waves;
> earth was unknown
> and heaven above
> only Ginnungagap[1]
> was — there was no grass.'

Then Just-as-high said: 'It was many æons before the earth was created that Niflheim was made, and in the midst of it is a well called Hvergelmir,[2] and thence flow the rivers with these names: Svöl,[3] Gunnthrá,[4] Fjörm, Fimbulthul,[5] Slíð,[6] Hríð,[7] Sylg, Ylg, Víð,[8] Leipt[9] and Gjöll which is next Hel's gate.'

Then Third said: 'The first world to exist, however, was Muspell in the southern hemisphere; it is light and hot and that region flames and burns so that those who do not belong to it and whose native land it is not, cannot endure it. The one who sits there at land's end to guard it is called Surt; he has a flaming sword, and at the end of the world he will come and harry and will vanquish all the gods and burn the whole world with fire. As it says in the *Sibyl's Vision*:

> Surt from the south comes
> with spoiler of twigs[10]
> blazing his sword
> [like] sun of the Mighty Ones:
> mountains will crash down,
> troll-women stumble,
> men tread the road to Hel,
> heaven's rent asunder.'

1 Open Void.	4 Battle-defiant.	7 Storming.
2 Bubbling Cauldron.	5 Loud-bubbling.	8 Broad.
3 Cool.	6 Fearsome.	9 Fast-as-lightning.
		10 Fire.

Gangleri asked: 'How were things arranged before families came into existence or mankind increased?'

High One said: 'When those rivers which are called Élivágar[1] came so far from their source that the yeasty venom accompanying them hardened like slag, it turned into ice. Then when that ice formed and was firm, a drizzling rain that arose from the venom poured over it and cooled into rime, and one layer of ice formed on top of the other throughout Ginnungagap.'

Then Just-as-high said: 'That part of Ginnungagap which turned northwards became full of the ice and the hoar frost's weight and heaviness, and within there was drizzling rain and gusts of wind. But the southern part of Ginnungagap became light by meeting the sparks and glowing embers which flew out of the world of Muspell.'

Then Third said: 'Just as cold and all harsh things emanated from Niflheim, so everything in the neighbourhood of Muspell was warm and bright. Ginnungagap was as mild as windless air, and where the soft air of the heat met the frost so that it thawed and dripped, then, by the might of that which sent the heat, life appeared in the drops of running fluid and grew into the likeness of a man. He was given the name Ymir, but the frost ogres call him Aurgelmir, and that is where the families of frost ogres come from, as is said in the *Shorter Sibyl's Vision*:

> All the sibyls
> are from Viðólf,
> all the wizards from Vilmeið,
> but the sorcerers from Svarthöfði,
> all the giants have come
> from Ymir.

And here is what the giant Vafthrúðnir[2] said [in answer to Óðin's question]:

---

1 Rivers-whipped-by-passing-showers.   2 Strong-in-difficult-riddles.

Whence first from giant-kin
came Aurgelmir the well-informed?
From the Élivágar
oozed drops of venom
that grew till they fashioned a giant,
all our kindred came from thence,
because of this birth
they are aye far too barbarous.'

Then Gangleri said: 'How did families grow thence? How was it arranged that men became numerous? Do you believe it was a god you were speaking about just now?'

High One replied: 'In no wise do we consider he was a god. He and all his family were evil; we call them frost ogres. But it is said that while he slept he fell into a sweat; then there grew under his left arm a man and woman, and one of his legs got a son with the other, and that is where the families of frost ogres come from. We call that old frost ogre Ymir.'

Then Gangleri said: 'Where was Ymir's home, and what did he live on?'

[High One replied:] 'As soon as the frost thawed, it became a cow called Auðhumla, and four rivers of milk ran from her teats, and she fed Ymir.'

Then Gangleri asked: 'What did the cow live on?'

High One answered: 'She licked the ice-blocks which were salty, and by the evening of the first day of the block-licking appeared a man's hair, on the second day a man's head, and on the third day the whole man was there. He was called Buri. He was handsome and tall and strong. He had a son called Bor, who married a woman called Bestla, daughter of the giant Bölthorn. They had three sons; the first Óðin; the second, Vili; the third, Vé; and it is my belief that that Óðin, in association with his brothers, is the ruler of heaven and earth. We think that that is his title; it is the name given to the man we know to be greatest and most famous, and you can take it that that is his [Óðin's] title.'

Then Gangleri asked: 'How did they get on together? Was one group more powerful than the other?'

Then High One answered: 'Bor's sons killed the giant Ymir, and when he fell, so much blood poured from his wounds that they drowned the whole tribe of frost ogres with it — except for one who escaped with his household; this one is known to the giants as Bergelmir. He climbed up on to his "lur"[1] and his wife with him, and there they were safe. From them spring the families of frost ogres, as it is said here:

> Innumerable years ago,
> before the earth was made,
> was born the giant Bergelmir;
> the first thing I remember
> was when they laid
> that wise one down on a "lur".'

Then Gangleri said: 'What did the sons of Bor do next, since you believe they are gods?'

High One said: 'There is a great deal to be told about this. They took Ymir and carried him into the middle of Ginnungagap, and made the world from him: from his blood the sea and lakes, from his flesh the earth, from his bones the mountains; rocks and pebbles they made from his teeth and jaws and those bones that were broken.'

Just-as-high said: 'From the blood which welled freely from his wounds they fashioned the ocean, when they put together the earth and girdled it, laying the ocean round about it. To cross it would strike most men as impossible.'

Third added: 'They also took his skull and made the sky from it and set it over the earth with its four sides, and under each corner they put a dwarf. These are called: East, West, North, and South. Then they took the sparks and burning embers that were flying about after they had been blown out of Muspell, and placed them in the midst of Ginnungagap to give light to heaven

1 Boat, made from a hollowed-out tree-trunk; it can also mean 'coffin'.

above and earth beneath. They gave their stations to all the stars, some fixed in the sky; others [planetary] that had wandered at will in the firmament were now given their appointed places and the paths in which they were to travel. So it is said in ancient poems that from that time sprang the reckoning of days and years, as it is said in the *Sibyl's Vision*:

> The sun did not know
> where she had her home,
> the moon did not know
> what might he had,
> stars did not know
> where their stations were.

Thus it was before this was done.'

Then Gangleri said: 'Great tidings I'm hearing now. That was a marvellous piece of craftsmanship, and skilfully contrived. How was the earth fashioned?'

Then High One answered: 'It is round, and surrounding it lies the deep sea, and on the strand of that sea they gave lands to the families of giants to settle, but inland they [Bor's sons] built a stronghold round the world on account of the hostility of the giants; for this stronghold they used Ymir's eyebrows, and they called it Miðgarð. They took his brains too and flung them up into the air and made from them the clouds, as it is said here:

> From Ymir's flesh
> the earth was made
> and from his blood the seas,
> crags from his bones,
> trees from his hair,
> and from his skull the sky.
>
> From his eyebrows
> the blessed gods
> made Miðgarð for the sons of men,
> and from his brains
> were created
> all storm-threatening clouds.'

Then Gangleri said: 'It seems to me they made great progress when heaven and earth were created and the sun and the stars given their stations and arrangements made for day and night, but whence came the men who inhabit the world?'

Then High One answered: 'When they were going along the sea-shore, the sons of Bor found two trees and they picked these up and created men from them. The first gave them spirit and life; the second, understanding and power of movement; the third, form, speech, hearing and sight. They gave them clothes and names. The man was called Ask[1] and the woman Embla;[2] and from them have sprung the races of men who were given Miðgarð to live in. Next they built a stronghold for themselves in the middle of the world, which is called Ásgarð — we call it Troy. There the gods and their kindred lived, and from then on came to pass many events and memorable happenings both in heaven and earth. There is a place there called Hliðskjálf,[3] and when Óðin sat there on his high seat he saw over the whole world and what everyone was doing, and he understood everything he saw. His wife, the daughter of Fjörgvin, was named Frigg, and from that family has come the kindred that inhabited ancient Ásgarð and those kingdoms belonging to it; we call the members of that family the Æsir and they are all divinities. He [Óðin] may well be called All-father for this reason — he is the father of all the gods and men and of everything that he and his power created. The earth was his daughter and his wife; by her he had his first son, Ása-Thór. Might and strength were Thór's characteristics, by these he dominates every living creature.

'There was a giant living in Giantland called Nörfi or Narfi. He had a daughter named Night. She was dark and swarthy, like the family to which she belonged. Her first marriage was with a man called Naglfari, their son was called Auð. Next she was married to Annar, their daughter was called Earth. Last, Delling[4]

---

1 Ash-tree.
2 Elm?
3 Hall-of-many-doors or Hall-with-one-big-doorway.
4 Shining One.

married her, and he was of the family of the gods. Their son was Day, he was bright and beautiful like his father's side. Then All-father took Night and her son, Day, and gave them two horses and two chariots and put them up in the sky, so that they should ride round the world every twenty-four hours. Night rides first on a horse called Hrímfaxi,[1] and every morning he be-dews the earth with the foam from his bit. Day's horse is called Skin-faxi,[2] and the whole earth and sky are illumined by his mane.'

Then Gangleri said: 'How does he guide the course of the sun and moon?'

High One replied: 'There was a man called Mundilfari who had two children. They were so fair and beautiful that he called one of them Moon and the other, a daughter, Sun; he married her to a man called Glen. The gods, however, were angered at his arrogance and took the brother and sister and put them up in the sky. They made Sun drive the horses which drew the chariot of the sun that the gods had made to light the worlds from a spark which flew from Muspell. The horses are called Árvak and Alsvið.[3] Under the shoulder-blades of the horses the gods put two bellows to cool them, and in some poems that is called iron-cold.[4] Moon governs the journeying of the moon and decides the time of its waxing and waning. He took from earth two children, known as Bil and Hjúki, as they were coming away from the spring called Byrgir carrying on their shoulders the pail called Sœg and the pole Símul. Their father's name is Viðfinn. These children accompany Moon, as may be seen from earth.'

Then Gangleri said: 'The sun moves fast and almost as if she were afraid; she could not travel faster if she were in fear of her life.'

Then High One answered: 'It is not surprising that she goes at a great pace; her pursuer is close behind her and there is nothing she can do but flee.'

1 Frosty-mane.
2 Shining-mane.
3 Early-waker and All-strong.
4 Literally 'iron-coal'.

Then Gangleri asked: 'Who is it that torments her like this?'

High One replied: 'There are two wolves, and the one pursuing her who is called Skoll is the one she fears; he will [ultimately] catch her. The other that runs in front of her, however, is called Hati Hróðvitnisson, and he wants to catch the moon and will in the end.'

Then Gangleri asked: 'What family do the wolves come from?'

High One said: 'To the east of Miðgarð in a forest called Iron Wood lives a giantess. Troll women known as Ironwoodites live in that forest. The aged giantess gave birth to many giant sons, all of them in the shape of wolves, and these two wolves have come about in that way. It is said that the one called Mánagarm[1] became the most powerful member of that family; he gorges on the flesh of all who die, and he will swallow the moon and bespatter the sky and all the air with blood. Because of this the sun will lose its brightness, and the winds will then become wild and rage on every side. As it says in the *Sibyl's Vision*:

> The ancient one lives in the east
> in the Wood of Iron
> and there gives birth
> to Fenrir's brood;
> one of them all
> especially
> in form of a troll
> will seize the sun.
>
> He is gorged with the flesh
> of the death-doomed
> and with red blood he reddens
> the dwellings of the gods;
> sunlight of summers to come
> will be black
> and all weathers bad —
> Do you know any more or not?'

Then Gangleri asked: 'What is the way from earth to heaven?'

1 Moon's Dog.

Then High One answered, laughing: 'No one well informed would ask such a question. Have you never been told that the gods built a bridge from earth to heaven called Bifröst?[1] You will have seen it, [but] maybe you call it the rainbow. It has three colours and is very strong, and made with more skill and cunning than other structures. But strong as it is, it will break when the sons of Muspell ride out over it to harry, and their horses [will] swim over great rivers; and in this fashion they will come on the scene.'

Then Gangleri said: 'It doesn't seem to me that the gods built a reliable bridge when it is going to break, and [yet] they can do what they will.'

High One said: 'The gods are not to blame for this structure. Bifröst is a good bridge, but there is nothing in this world that can be relied on when the sons of Muspell are on the warpath.'

Then Gangleri asked: 'What did All-father set about doing, once Ásgarð was built?'

High One replied: 'At first he appointed rulers who, along with him, were to control the destinies of men, and decide how the stronghold should be governed. That was in the place called Iðavöll[2] in the middle of the stronghold. Their first task was to build a temple in which there were seats for the twelve of them, apart from the high-seat of the All-father. That is the largest and best dwelling on earth; outside and in it is like pure gold; it is called Glaðsheim.[3] They built another hall that was the sanctuary of the goddesses, and it was a very beautiful building; it is called Vingólf. Next they laid the hearth of a forge and then made hammer and tongs and an anvil, and thenceforward all other tools, and went on to work in metals and stone and wood, and also in gold, so abundantly that all their household utensils and furniture were of gold. That age was called the Golden Age before it was spoiled by the arrival of the women who came from Giantland.

1 Quivering Roadway.
2 Plain-that-renews-itself or Plain-of-activity.
3 Radiant Home.

'Then the gods seated themselves on their thrones and held counsel, and remembered how dwarfs had quickened in the earth and under the soil like maggots in flesh. The dwarfs had first emerged and come to life in Ymir's flesh, and at that time were maggots. But by the decree of the gods they acquired human understanding and the appearance of men, although they lived in the earth and in rocks. Móðsognir was the most famous, and next to him Durin. As it says in the *Sibyl's Vision*:

> All the gods sought then
> their judgment-seats,
> powers that are supreme
> decided how dwarfs
> should be brought into being
> from bloody surf
> and the legs of Bláin.[1]

> There many dwarfs
> resembling men
> they made in earth
> as Durin said.

And the sibyl gives these as their names:

> Nýi, Niði,
> Norðri,[2] Suðri,[3]
> Austri,[4] Vestri,[5]
> Althjóf, Dvalin,[6]
> Nár,[7] Náin,
> Niping, Dáin,
> Bifur, Báfur,
> Bömbör, Nori,
> [Óri],[8] Ónar,
> Óin, Mjöðvitnir,[9]
> Vig and Ganndálf,[10]
> Vinndálf,[11] Thorin,[12]

[handwritten note: Tolkien used these as names for the dwarves (esp in Hobbit)]

[1] Ymir's bones?
[2] North.
[3] South.
[4] East.
[5] West.
[6] One-lying-in-a-trance.
[7] Corpse.
[8] Raging One.
[9] Mead-wolf.
[10] Sorcerer-elf.
[11] Wind-elf.
[12] Bold One.

Fili, Kili,
Fundin,[1] Vali,
Thrór, Thróin,
Thekk,[2] Lit, Vit,
Nýr,[3] Nýráð,
Rekk, Ráðsvið.[4]

And these too are dwarfs and they live in rocks, but the above-mentioned live in the earth:

Draupnir, Dólgthvari,[5]
Haur, Hugstari,
Hleðjólf, Glóin,
Dóri, Óri,
Dúf, Andvari,
Heptifili,
Hár,[6] Svíar.

The following, however, came from Svarin's grave-mound to Aurvangar in Jöruvellir, and from these have sprung Lovar; their names are

Skirvir, Virvir,
Skafið, Ái,
Álf, Ingi,
Eikinskjaldi,[7]
Fal, Frosti,
Fið, Ginnar.'[8]

Then Gangleri asked: 'Where is the chief place or sanctuary of the gods?'

High One replied: 'It is by the ash Yggdrasil. There every day the gods have to hold a court.'

Then Gangleri asked: 'In what way is that place famous?'

Then Just-as-high said: 'The ash is the best and greatest of all trees; its branches spread out over the whole world and reach up over heaven. The tree is held in position by three roots that

1 Found One.	4 Wise-in-advice.	7 With-oak-shield.
2 Pleasant One.	5 Battle-stock.	8 Enticer.
3 New One.	6 Tall One.	

spread far out; one is among the Æsir, the second among the frost ogres where once was Ginnungagap, and the third extends over Niflheim, and under that root is the well Hvergelmir; but Níðhögg[1] gnaws at the root from below. Under the root that turns in the direction of the frost ogres lies the spring of Mímir, in which is hidden wisdom and understanding; Mímir is the name of the owner of the spring. He is full of wisdom because he drinks [water] from the spring out of the horn Gjöll. All-father came there and asked for a single drink from the spring, but he did not get it until he had given one of his eyes as a pledge. As it says in the *Sibyl's Vision*:

> I know for certain Óðin
> where you concealed your eye,
> in the famous
> spring of Mímir;
> mead he drinks
> every morning
> from the pledge of the Father-of-the-slain.
> Do you know any more or not?

The third root of the ash tree is in the sky, and under that root is the very sacred spring called the Spring of Urð.[2] There the gods hold their court of justice. The Æsir ride up to that place every day over the bridge Bifröst, which is also known as the Bridge of the Æsir. The names of the horses of the gods are as follows: Sleipnir is the best, Óðin owns him, he has eight legs; the second is Glað;[3] the third, Gyllir; the fourth, Glen; the fifth, Skeið-brimir;[4] the sixth, Silfr[in]topp;[5] the seventh, Sinir;[6] the eighth, Gils; the ninth, Falhófnir;[7] the tenth, Gulltopp;[8] the eleventh, Léttfet[i].[9] Baldr's horse was burned with him, and Thór walks to the court wading through the rivers that have these names:

1 Striker-that-destroys. 4 Fast-galloper.   7 Shaggy Fetlock.
2 Destiny.   5 Silver Forelock.   8 Golden Forelock.
3 Shining One.   6 Strong-of-sinew.   9 Lightfoot.

Körmt and Örmt
and both the Kerlaugar
these must Thór wade through
every day,
when he goes to give judgment
at Yggdrasil's ash,
since the Bridge of the Æsir
is flaming with fire
the sacred waters glow.'

Then Gangleri asked: 'Does fire burn over Bifröst?'

High One replied: 'The red you see in the rainbow is flaming fire. If it were possible for all who wanted to go over Bifröst to do so, the frost ogres and cliff giants would scale heaven. There are many beautiful places in heaven, and they are all under divine protection. There is a beautiful hall near the spring under the ash tree, and from it come three maidens whose names are Urð, Verðandi, Skuld.[1] These maidens shape the lives of men, and we call them Norns. There are, however, more Norns, those that come to every child that is born in order to shape its life, and these are beneficent, others belong to the family of the elves and a third group belongs to the family of the dwarfs, as it says here:

Of different origins
are the Norns, I think,
not all of one kindred;
some come from Æsir-kin,
some from the elves
and some are the daughters of Dvalin.'

Then Gangleri said: 'If the Norns decide the fates of men, they appoint very unequal destinies for them; for some have a good and abundant life, but others have little wealth or fame. Some have a long life and others a short one.'

High One said: 'The good Norns who come from good stock shape good lives, but those who meet with misfortune owe it to the evil Norns.'

1 Past, Present and Future.

Then Gangleri asked: 'In what other way is the ash tree remarkable?'

High One said: 'There is a great deal to tell about it. In the branches of the ash sits an eagle, and it is very knowledgeable, and between its eyes sits a hawk called Veðrfölnir.[1] A squirrel called Ratatosk[2] springs up and down the ash tree and conveys words of abuse exchanged between the eagle and Niðhögg. Four harts leap about the branches of the ash and eat the shoots; these are their names: Dáin, Dvalin, Duneyr, Durathrór. And along with Niðhögg in Hvergelmir there are so many serpents that no tongue can count them. As it says here:

> The ash Yggdrasil
> endures more pain
> than men perceive,
> the hart devours it from above
> and the sides of it decay,
> Niðhögg is gnawing from below.

It is said:

> There are more serpents
> under the ash
> Yggdrasil than fools imagine,
> Góin[3] and Móin[4]
> Grafvitnir's[5] sons,
> Grábak[6] and Grafvölluð[7]
> Ófnir and Sváfnir,
> I think that they will destroy
> for ever that ash-tree's branches.

It is said further that the Norns who live near the spring of Urð draw water from the spring every day, and along with it the clay that lies round about the spring, and they besprinkle the ash so that its branches shall not wither or decay. But that water is so

---

1 Weather-bleached One. 4 Dweller-on-a-moor. 6 Grey-back.
2 Gnaw-tooth. 5 Grave-wolf. 7 Field-burrower.
3 Living-deep-in-earth.

45

sacred that everything that comes into the spring becomes as white as the film (which is called "skin") that lies within the egg-shell. As it says here:

> I know an ash-tree
> known as Yggdrasil,
> tall tree and sacred
> besprent with white clay,
> thence come the dews
> that fall in the dales;
> it stands ever green
> over Urð's spring.

The dew which falls from it to the earth is called honey-dew by men, and the bees feed on it. Two birds are nourished in the spring of Urð; they are called swans, and from them have come the birds of this name.'

Then Gangleri said: 'You have a great deal to tell concerning heaven. Are there any other important places besides the spring of Urð?'

High One answered: 'There are many magnificent places there. There is one called Álfheim, and there live the people called the light elves, but the dark elves live down in the earth and they are unlike the others in appearance and much more so in character. The light elves are fairer than the sun to look upon, but the dark elves, blacker than pitch. Then there is Breiðablik,[1] there is no place there more beautiful. There is also one called Glitnir,[2] and its walls and posts and pillars are of red gold, but its roof is silver. Further there is that place called Himinbjörg;[3] it is at heaven's end by the bridge-head where Bifröst joins heaven. There is, moreover, a great dwelling called Valaskjálf[4] owned by Óðin, which the gods built and roofed with pure silver. The high seat known as Hliðskjálf is there in this hall, and when All-father sits on this seat he sees over the whole world. In the southern end

---

1 Gleaming-far-and-wide.
2 Radiant Place.
3 Mount-of-heaven.
4 Hall-of-the-slain.

of heaven is the most beautiful hall of all, brighter than the sun;
it is called Gimlé;[1] it shall stand when both heaven and earth
have passed away, and good and righteous men will inhabit that
place for all time. As it says in the *Sibyl's Vision*:

> I know where stands a hall
> brighter than sunlight
> better than gold
> in Lee-of-flame, Gimlé;
> hosts of the righteous
> shall it inherit,
> live in delight
> everlastingly.'

Then Gangleri asked: 'What will protect this place when Surt's
Fire is burning heaven and earth?'

High One replied: 'It is said that there is another heaven to the
south of and above this one, and it is called Andlang;[2] and there
is yet a third heaven above these ones which is called Viðbláin,[3]
and we think that this place [Gimlé] is there. At present, however,
we think that it is inhabited only by white elves.'

Then Gangleri asked: 'Where does the wind come from? It is
so strong that it stirs up great seas and fans fire into flame yet,
strong as it is, it can never be seen, so marvellously is it made.'

High One said: 'I can easily tell you that. At the northern end
of the sky sits the giant called Hræsvelg.[4] He has the form of an
eagle, and when he spreads his wings for flight a wind arises from
under them, as it says here:

> The one who squats at the end of the sky
> is known as Engulfer-of-corpses
> a giant in eagle form;
> they say from his wings
> comes the wind
> of this world.'

Then Gangleri asked: 'Why is there such a difference between
hot summer and cool winter?'

1 Lee-of-fire.   2 Outstretched.   3 Wide Blue.   4 Corpse-swallower.

High One said: 'A well-informed man would not ask this. Everyone knows why. However, if you are the only person so ill-informed as never to have heard, I'll admit it is better for you to ask once in your foolishness than for you to go on any longer in ignorance of what you ought to know. The father of Summer is called Svásuð,[1] and he has such a joyous life that whatever is pleasant is called so from him. But Winter's father is called by turns Vindlóni or Vindsval.[2] He is the son of Vásað;[3] these kinsmen are grim and cold-hearted and Winter has their disposition.'

Then Gangleri asked: 'Who are the gods men ought to believe in?'

High One replied: 'The divine gods are twelve in number.'

Just-as-high added: 'The goddesses are no less sacred and no less powerful.'

Then Third said: 'Óðin is the highest and the oldest of the gods. He rules all things and, no matter how mighty the other gods may be, they all serve him as children do their father. His wife is Frigg and she knows the fates of all men, although she does not prophesy, as is said here, when Óðin himself was speaking to that god known as Loki:

> You're insane, Loki,
> and out of your senses,
> Loki, why don't you desist?
> I think that Frigg
> knows the whole of fate
> although she herself says nothing.

Óðin is called All-father because he is the father of all the gods. He is also called Valfather because all who fall in battle are his adopted sons. He allots to them Valhalla and Vingólf, and then they are called Einherjar.[4] He is also called Hangaguð,[5] Haptaguð,[6] Farmaguð,[7] and he named himself in many other ways when he came to King Geirröð:

1 Agreeable.   3 Damp Cold.   5 God-of-the-hanged.   7 God-of-
2 Wind-cool.   4 Belonging-to-an-army.   6 God-of-the-gods.   cargoes.

I am called Grím[1]
And Gangleri,
Herjan,[2] Hjálmberi,[3]
Thekk,[4] Thriði,[5]
Thuð,[6] Uð,
Helblindi,[7] Hár,[8]
Sað, Svipall,[9]
Sanngetall,[10]
Herteit,[11] Hnikar,[12]
Bileyg,[13] Báleyg,[14]
Bölverk,[15] Fjölnir,
Grímnir,[16] Glapsvið, Fjölsvið,[17]
Síðhött,[18] Síðskegg,[19]
Sigföð,[20] Hnikuð,[21]
Allföð,[22] Atríð, Farmatýr,[23]
Óski,[24] Ómi,
Jafnhár,[25] Biflindi,
Göndlir, Hárbarð,[26]
Sviður, Sviðrir,
Jálk, Kjalar, Viður,
Thrór, Ygg,[27] Thund,
Vak,[28] Skilving,
Váfuð, Hroptatýr,
Gaut, Veratýr.'[29]

Then Gangleri said: 'You have given him a tremendous number of names and, upon my word, it would show great learning to know and cite in each instance the events that had given rise to them.'

Then High One said: 'It would take a vast amount of knowledge to go over them all. It will, however, be quickest to tell

1 Masked One.
2 Raider.
3 Helmeted One.
4 Pleasant One.
5 Third.
6 Thin One.
7 One-who-blinds-with death.
8 High One.
9 Changeable One.
10 One-who-guesses-right.
11 Glad-of-war.
12 [Spear-]thruster.
13 One-whose-eye-deceives-him, i.e. one-eyed.
14 Flame-eyed One.
15 Worker-of-evil.
16 Masked One.
17 Very-wise One.
18 Deep-hooded One.
19 Long-bearded One.
20 Father-of-battle.
21 [Spear-]thruster.
22 All-father.
23 Cargo-god.
24 Fulfiller-of-desire.
25 Just-as-high.
26 Grey-bearded One.
27 Terrible One.
28 Alert One.
29 God-of-men.

you that most of these names have been given him because the
many different nations in the world, all speaking different
tongues, felt the need of translating his name into their several
languages in order to worship and pray to him. Some incidents
giving rise to these names, however, took place on his journeys,
and these have been made into tales, and it will be impossible for
you to be called a well-informed person if you cannot relate
some of these great events.'

Then Gangleri asked: 'What are the names of the other gods?
How do they occupy themselves? What have they done to
distinguish themselves?'

High One said: 'Thór, who is called Ása-Thór or Thór-the-
charioteer, is the foremost of them. He is strongest of all gods
and men. He rules over that kingdom called Thrúðvangar,[1] and
his hall is called Bilskirnir;[2] in that building are six hundred and
forty floors — it is the largest house known to men. As it says in
the *Lay of Grímnir*:

> Bilskirnir with its winding ways
> I know has more
> than six hundred and forty floors,
> of those buildings
> I know to be roofed
> I know my son's is the largest.

Thór has two goats known as Tooth-gnasher and Gap-tooth, and
the chariot he drives in. The goats pull the chariot, and for this
reason he is called Thór-the-charioteer. He also owns three
precious things. One is the hammer Mjöllnir,[3] which the frost
ogres and cliff giants know when it is raised aloft, and that is not
surprising since he has cracked the skulls of many of their kith
and kin. His second great treasure is a belt of strength, and when
he buckles that on his divine might is doubled. And he owns a
third thing of great value in his iron gauntlets; he cannot do

1 Plains-of-power.   2 Strong.   3 Crusher.

without these when he grips the handle of the hammer. But no one is well-informed enough to be able to recount all his mighty deeds. I can, however, tell you so many things about him that it would take a long time before all I knew had been related.'

Then Gangleri said: 'I would like to hear about more of the gods.'

High One said: 'Another son of Óðin's is called Baldr, and there is [nothing but] good to be told of him. He is the best of them and everyone sings his praises. He is so fair of face and bright that a splendour radiates from him, and there is one flower so white that it is likened to Baldr's brow; it is the whitest of all flowers. From that you can tell how beautiful his body is, and how bright his hair. He is the wisest of the gods, and the sweetest-spoken, and the most merciful, but it is a characteristic of his that once he has pronounced a judgment it can never be altered. He lives in the place in heaven called Breiðablik; nothing impure can be there, as it says here:

> There where Baldr
> has built his dwellings
> they call it Breiðablik;
> in that land
> where I know
> there are fewest evil things.

'The third god is the one called Njörð. He lives in heaven at a place called Nóatún.[1] He controls the path of the wind, stills sea and fire, and is to be invoked for seafaring and fishing. He is so wealthy and prosperous that he is able to bestow abundance of land and property on those who call on him for this. (Njörð is not one of the Æsir.) He was brought up in Vanaheim, but the Vanir gave him as a hostage to the gods and accepted as a counter-hostage one called Hœnir. He brought about a reconciliation between the gods and the Vanir.

'Njörð has a wife called Skaði, daughter of the giant Thjazi.

1 Ship-yard.

51

Skaði wanted to have the homestead her father had had, on some mountains in the place called Thrymheim,[1] but Njörð wanted to be near the sea. They came to an agreement that they should be nine nights in Thrymheim and then another nine at Nóatún. When Njörð came back to Nóatún from the mountain, however, he said this:

> Mountains I loathed,
> no longer than nine
> nights did I stay there,
> the howling of wolves
> seemed ugly to me
> compared with the hooping of swans.

Then Skaði said this:

> I could not sleep
> by the shore of the sea
> for the noise of the mew
> that awakened me,
> the bird that flew
> each dawn from the deep.

'Then Skaði went up the mountain and lived in Thrymheim, and she goes about a great deal on skis and with her bow and arrow shoots wild animals. She is called Snow-shoe goddess, or Snow-shoe divinity. As it is said:

> Thrymheim's the name
> of Thjazi's place
> that giant of monstrous frame;
> his daughter wed with one of the gods
> Skaði, now, the fair of face,
> lives there in her sire's old home.

'Njörð of Nóatún had two children after this, a son called Frey[2] and a daughter Freyja.[3] They were beautiful to look at, and powerful. Frey is an exceedingly famous god; he decides when the sun shall shine or the rain come down, and along with that

1 Storm-home.   2 Lord.   3 Lady.

the fruitfulness of the earth, and he is good to invoke for peace and plenty. He also brings about the prosperity of men. But Freyja is the most renowned of the goddesses. She owns that homestead in heaven known as Fólkvangar,[1] and whenever she rides into battle she has half the slain and Óðin half, as it says here:

> Fólkvangar's where
> Freyja decides
> who shall sit where in the hall;
> half the slain every day
> she chooses
> and Óðin has half.

'Her hall Sessrúmnir[2] is large and beautiful. When she goes on a journey she sits in a chariot drawn by two cats. She is most readily invoked, and from her name derives the polite custom of calling the wives of men of rank Frú.[3] She enjoys love poetry, and it is good to call on her for help in love affairs.'

Then Gangleri said: 'The Æsir appear to me to be very powerful, and it is not surprising that you have great authority, since you possess such understanding of the gods and know how each should be prayed to. Are there more gods still?'

High One said: 'There is a god called Týr. He is the boldest and most courageous, and has power over victory in battle; it is good for brave men to invoke him. It is a proverbial saying that he who surpasses others and does not waver is "Týr-valiant". He is also so well informed that a very knowledgeable man is said to be "Týr-wise". Here is one proof of his daring. When the gods tried to persuade the wolf Fenrir to allow the fetter Gleipnir to be placed on him, he did not believe that they would free him until they put Týr's hand in his mouth as a pledge. Then, when the Æsir would not loose him, he bit off the hand at the place now known as the "wolf-joint".[4] [So Týr] is one-handed and he is not called a peace-maker.

'One [god] is called Bragi. He is famous for wisdom and most

1 Field-of-warriors. 2 With-many-seats. 3 Madam. 4 The wrist.

of all for eloquence and skill with words; he knows most about poetry, and from him poetry gets its name,[1] and from his name the man or woman who can use words better than others is called a poet. His wife is Iðun.[2] She keeps in her box the apples the gods have to eat, when they grow old, to become young again, and so it will continue up to Ragnarök.'[3]

Then Gangleri said: 'It seems to me that the gods trust rather a lot to the care and good faith of Iðun.'

Then High One answered, laughing: 'It did nearly result in misfortune once. I can tell you more about that, but first you shall hear the names of more of the gods.

'One is called Heimdall. He is called the white god, and he is great and holy. Nine maidens gave birth to him, and all of them sisters. He is also known as Hallinskíði and Goldtooth, he had teeth of gold. His horse is called Goldtuft. He lives in a place called Himinbjörg[4] by Bifröst. He is the warden of the gods, and sits there at the end of heaven to guard the bridge from the cliff giants. He needs less sleep than a bird, and can see a hundred leagues in front of him as well by night as by day. He can hear the grass growing on the earth and the wool on sheep, and everything that makes more noise. He has the trumpet known as the horn Gjöll, and its blast can be heard over all the worlds. A name for the head is Heimdall's sword. So it is said:

> Himinbjörg's said to be
> the name of Heimdall's house;
> there the warden of the gods
> glad
> in his gracious home
> drinks the good mead.

And further he says himself in *Heimdall's Spell*:

> Of nine mothers I'm the son
> and son of nine sisters too.

1 One of the Old Icelandic words for poetry is *bragr*.
2 One-who-renews.   3 The Twilight of the Gods.   4 Cliffs-of-heaven.

'Höð is one of the gods. He is blind. He is immensely strong too, but the gods would rather there were no need to mention his name, since his handiwork will long be remembered amongst gods and men.

'Víðar is the name of one of them, the silent god. He has a stout shoe and is almost as strong as Thór. The gods rely greatly on him in all difficult situations.

'Áli or Váli is the name of one, a son of Óðin and Rind; he is bold in battle and a very good shot.

'Ull, Sif's son and Thór's stepson, is one [too]. He is such a good archer and ski-runner that no one can rival him. He is beautiful to look at as well and he has all the characteristics of a warrior. It is also good to call on him in duels.

'Forseti is the son of Baldr and Nanna, Nep's daughter. He owns the hall in heaven known as Glitnir. Without exception all who come to him with legal disputes go away reconciled; that is the best court known to gods and men. As it says here:

> There's a hall called Glitnir
> with pillars of gold
> it's also roofed with silver;
> there Forseti
> spends all day long
> settling all suits-at-law.

'Also reckoned amongst the gods is one that some call the mischiefmonger of the Æsir and the father-of-lies and the disgrace-of-gods-and-men. He is the son of the giant Fárbauti and his name is Loki or Lopt. His mother's name is Laufey or Nál, and Býleist and Helblindi are his brothers. Loki is handsome and fair of face, but has an evil disposition and is very changeable of mood. He excelled all men in the art of cunning, and he always cheats. He was continually involving the Æsir in great difficulties and he often helped them out again by guile. His wife's name is Sigyn; their son [is] Nari or Narvi.

'Loki had still more children. There was a giantess in Giantland called Angrboða.[1] Loki had three children by her, the first was the wolf Fenrir, the second, Jörmungand — that is the Miðgarð Serpent — and the third, Hel. Now when the gods knew that these three children were being brought up in Giantland and had gathered from prophecy that they would meet with great harm and misfortune on their account (and they all anticipated evil, first from the mother and still worse from the father), All-father sent some of the gods to capture the children and bring them to him. And when they came to him, he flung the serpent into the deep sea which surrounds the whole world, and it grew so large that it now lies in the middle of the ocean round the earth, biting its own tail. He threw Hel into Niflheim and gave her authority over nine worlds, on the condition that she shared all her provisions with those who were sent to her, namely men who die from disease or old age. She has a great homestead there with extraordinarily high walls and huge gates. Her hall is called Éljúðnir;[2] her plate, Hunger; her knife, Famine; her manservant, Ganglati;[3] her maid-servant, Ganglöt;[4] the stone at the entrance, Drop-to-destruction; her bed, Sick-bed; its hangings, Glimmering Misfortune. Hel is half black, half flesh-colour, and is easily recognized from this; she looks rather grim and gloomy.

'The gods brought the wolf up at home, and only Týr had the courage to go up to it and give it food. But when the gods saw how fast it was growing daily, and all prophecies foretold that it was doomed to do them injury, the Æsir adopted the plan of making a very strong fetter which they called Lœðing, and they took it to the wolf and bade him try his strength against it. But the wolf thought that it would not be too difficult for him [to snap it] and allowed them to do as they would; and the first time the wolf strained against it the fetter broke, so he got free from Lœðing.

---

1 Boder-of-sorrow.   3 Slow-moving.
2 Damp-with-sleet.   4 Slow-moving.

'Then the Æsir made another fetter twice as strong, which they called Drómi, and bade the wolf test himself again against that fetter, saying that he would become very famous for strength if such a strong chain would not hold him. The wolf, however, was thinking that, although the fetter was very strong, he had grown in might since he had broken Lœðing; it also occurred to him that he would have to expose himself to danger in order to become famous, so he let the fetter be put on him. When the Æsir said they were ready, he shook himself, knocking the fetter against the ground, and struggled against it, digging his feet in so hard that the fetter broke into pieces which flew far and wide; so he got himself out of Drómi. It has since become a proverb when anything is extraordinarily difficult that one gets loose from Lœðing or battles out of Drómi.

'After that the Æsir feared that they would never be able to get the wolf bound. Then All-father sent one called Skírnir, Frey's messenger, down to the World-of-dark-elves to some dwarfs, and had made the fetter called Gleipnir. This was made from six things: the noise a cat makes when it moves, the beard of a woman, the roots of a mountain, the sinews of a bear, the breath of a fish, and the spittle of a bird. Now, although you may not have known this before, you can easily prove that you are not being told a falsehood, since you will have observed that a woman has no beard, a cat makes no noise when running, a mountain has no roots and, upon my word, everything I have told you is just as true, although there are some things that you can't put to the test.'

Then Gangleri said: 'I can certainly understand it's true. I can see [that from] these things you have taken as examples, but how was the fetter made?'

High One replied: 'I can easily tell you that. The fetter was as smooth and soft as a ribbon of silk, but as trusty and strong as you are now going to hear. When the fetter was brought to the Æsir they thanked the messenger very much for carrying out his mission. Then the Æsir, calling to the wolf to go with them, went out on to an island called Lyngvi in a lake called Ámsvartnir. They showed him the silken band and bade him break it. They said it was a bit stronger than it appeared to be from its thickness and passed it from one to the other, testing its strength with their hands, and it did not break. They said, however, that the wolf would be able to snap it. The wolf's answer was: "This ribbon looks to me as if I could gain no renown from breaking it — it is so slight a cord; but if it has been made by guile and cunning, slender though it looks, it is not going to come on my legs." Then the gods said that he would soon snap so slight a ribbon of silk, when he had broken great fetters of iron before, "and if you don't succeed in snapping this cord you need not be afraid of the gods; we will set you free again." The wolf said: "If you bind me so that I can't get free, then you will sneak away so that it will be a long time before I get any help from you. I don't want to have that ribbon put on me. But rather than be accused of cowardice by you, let one of you place his hand in my mouth as a pledge that this is done in good faith." Each of the gods looked at the other then and thought that they were in a fix, and not one of them would stretch forth his hand, until Týr put out his right hand and laid it in the wolf's mouth. Now when the wolf began to struggle against it, the band tightened, and the more fiercely he struggled the firmer it got. They all laughed except Týr; he lost his hand. When the gods saw that the wolf was well and truly bound, they took the chain that was fast to this fetter and which was called Gelgja, and drawing it through a great boulder called Gjöll drove the boulder deep down into the earth. Then they took a huge stone called Thviti and sank it still deeper in the earth, and used this stone as a fastening peg. The wolf opened his mouth to a frightful width and struggled violently, wanting to bite them. Then they shoved a sword into his mouth so that the hilt was in its lower jaw and the point in the upper; that is his gag. He howls horribly, and the slaver running from his mouth forms the river called Vón.[1] There he will lie until Ragnarök.'

Then Gangleri said: 'Loki had very evil children, but all these brothers and sisters have great power. Why didn't the gods kill the wolf, since they anticipated evil from him?'

High One replied: 'The gods set such store by their sanctuary and temple that they would not pollute them with the wolf's blood, [even] although prophecies foretold that he would be the death of Óðin.'

Then Gangleri asked: 'What goddesses are there?'

High One replied: 'The foremost is Frigg. She owns that dwelling known as Fensalir, and it is most magnificent.

'Sága is another; she lives at Sökkvabekk, and that is a large estate.

'The third is Eir; she is the best of physicians.

'The fourth is Gefjon; she is a virgin, and women who die unmarried serve her.

'The fifth is Fulla; she, too, is a virgin and wears her hair loose and a golden band round her head. She carries Frigg's little box and looks after her shoes and knows her secrets.

'Freyja is as distinguished as Frigg. She is married to a man called Óð; their daughter is Hnoss; she is so lovely that whatever is beautiful and valuable is called "treasure" from her name.[2] Óð went away on long journeys and Freyja weeps for him, and her tears are red gold. Freyja has many names, and the reason for this is that she gave herself several when she went to look for Óð among peoples she did not know. She is called Mardöll and Hörn, Gefn[3] and Sýr.[4] Freyja owns the necklace of the Brísings. She is also called the divinity of the Vanir.

'The seventh goddess is Sjöfn; she is much concerned with turning the minds of people, both men and women, to love. From her name love is called *sjafni*.

'The eighth is Lofn; she is so gentle and good to invoke that she has permission from All-father and Frigg to bring together

1 Expectation. 2 The Old Icelandic for 'treasure' is *hnoss*. 3 Giver. 4 Sow.

men and women for whom marriage was forbidden or banned. From her name comes the word "permission", also what is much praised by men.

'The ninth is Vár; she listens to the vows and compacts made by men and women with each other; for this reason such agreements are called *várar*.[1] She also takes vengeance on those who break their vows.

'The tenth is Vör; she is so wise and searching that nothing can be concealed from her. It is a proverb that a woman becomes "aware" of what she gets to know.

'The eleventh is Syn;[2] she guards the door of the hall and shuts it against those who are not to enter. She is also appointed defending counsel at trials in cases she wishes to refute, hence the saying that "Syn is brought forward" when anyone denies an accusation.

'The twelfth is Hlín; she is appointed to protect those men Frigg wants to save from dangers, hence the proverb that "he who is protected 'leans' ".

'The thirteenth is Snotra; she is wise and gentle mannered. From her name a man or woman who is self-controlled is called *snotr*.[3]

'The fourteenth is Gná; Frigg sends her on her errands. She has a horse that runs through the air and over the sea called Hoofflourisher. Once when she was riding, some Vanir saw her riding in the air and one said:

> What is flying there,
> faring there
> and gliding through the air?

She answered:

> I am not flying,
> although I am faring
> gliding through the air
> on Hoof-flourisher
> whom Skinny-sides
> got by Breaker-of-fences.

1 Promises.   2 Denial.   3 Prudent.

'From Gná's name what soars high is called towering.

'Sól[1] and Bil are reckoned among the goddesses, but their nature has been described before.

'There are, moreover, others whose duty it is to serve in Valhalla, carry the drink round and look after the table service and ale-cups. Their names in the *Lay of Grímnir* are as follows:

> Hrist and Mist
> I want to bring me the horn,
> Skeggjöld and Skögul,
> Hild[2] and Thrúð,
> Hlökk[3] and Herfjötur,[4]
> Göll and Geirahöð,
> Randgríð[5] and Ráðgríð,
> and Reginleif.
> These bear ale to the Einherjar.

These are called Valkyries. Óðin sends them to every battle, and they choose death for the men destined to die, and award victory. Guð[6] and Rota and the youngest norn Skuld always ride to choose the slain and decide [the issue of] battles.

'Earth, the mother of Thór, and Rind, Váli's mother, are reckoned amongst the goddesses.

'There was a man called Gymir whose wife Aurboða was of the family of cliff giants. Their daughter is Gerð, who is an exceedingly beautiful woman. One day when Frey had gone to Hliðskjálf and was looking out over the whole world, he looked towards the north and saw in one place a large and beautiful dwelling. To this house went a woman; and, when she raised her arms to open the door, they illumined the sky and sea, and the whole world grew bright from her. So, for the presumption he had shown in seating himself on that holy seat, he paid by going away full of sorrow. When he came home, he neither spoke nor slept, nor did he drink anything, and no one dared to address him.

---

1 Sun.
2 Battle.
3 Din-of-battle.
4 Fetterer-of-an-army.
5 Shield-destroyer.
6 Conflict.

Then Njörð summoned Frey's chamberlain, Skírnir, and bade him go to Frey and ask him on whose account he was so angry that he would speak to no one. Skírnir said that he would go, but he was not eager and he said he expected an unpleasant answer from him. When he came to Frey, he asked him why he was so downcast that he would not speak with anyone. Then Frey replied, saying that he had seen a beautiful woman and on her account was so distressed that he would not live long if he could not obtain her. "And now you are to go" [he said], "and woo her for me and bring her here whether her father wishes it or not. I will reward you well for it." Skírnir answered saying that he would go on that errand, but Frey was to lend him his sword, which was such a good one that it fought by itself. Frey agreed to that and gave him the sword. Then Skírnir went and wooed the woman for him and obtained her promise that, nine nights later, she would come to a place called Barrey and there marry Frey. When, however, Skírnir told Frey the result of his mission, Frey said:

> One night is long,
> long is a second,
> how shall I three endure?
> shorter to me
> has a month often seemed
> than this half bridal-eve.

This was the reason why Frey had no weapon when he fought with Beli but killed him with a hart's horn.'

Then Gangleri said: 'It is very strange that a chieftain like Frey should give away a sword and leave himself without as good a one. It was a very great drawback to him when he fought with the man called Beli. Upon my word, he would regret his gift on that occasion.'

Then High One answered: 'It was a small affair when he and Beli met. Frey could have killed him with his [bare] hand[s]. The time will come when Frey will find it worse to be without a sword — when the sons of Muspell ride out to harry.'

Then Gangleri said: 'You say that all the men who have fallen in battle since the beginning of the world have now come to Óðin in Valhalla — what has he got to feed them with? I imagine that there must be a huge crowd of them there.'

Then High One replied: 'What you say is true. There is a huge crowd there, and there will be many more still, and yet they will seem too few when the wolf comes. But there is never so big a crowd in Valhalla that they don't get enough pork from the boar called Sæhrímnir. He is boiled every day, and comes alive every evening. But as for the question you are putting now, it seems to me that not many people would know enough to give you the correct answer. The cook's name is Andhrímnir,[1] and the cauldron is called Eldhrímnir,[2] as it is said here:

> Andhrímnir boils
> Valhalla's boar
> in the sooty cauldron,
> it's prime of pork
> but few men know
> on what Valhalla's champions feed.'

Then Gangleri asked: 'Does Óðin have the same food as the Einherjar?'

High One said: 'He gives what food is on his table to two wolves called Geri[3] and Freki;[4] but he himself needs nothing to eat. Wine is for him both food and drink, as it says here:

> Battle-wont and famous,
> Óðin war-glorious,
> sates Geri and Freki;
> the Father-of-armies
> himself lives always
> only on wine.

'Two ravens sit on his shoulders and bring to his ears all the news that they see or hear; they are called Hugin[5] and Munin.[6]

1 Sooty-face.	3 Greedy.	5 Thought.
2 Fire-sooty.	4 Gluttonous.	6 Memory.

He sends them out at daybreak to fly over the whole world, and they come back at breakfast-time; by this means he comes to know a great deal about what is going on, and on account of this men call him the god-of-ravens. As it is said:

> Over the world
> every day
> fly Hugin and Munin;
> I fear that Hugin
> will not come back,
> though I'm more concerned about Munin.'

Then Gangleri asked: 'What do the Einherjar have to drink in as much abundance as their food? Is water drunk there?'

Then High One said: 'That is a queer question to ask now — whether All-father who invites kings and earls and other men of rank gives them water to drink! It is my belief that many a one coming to Valhalla would think a drink of water dearly paid for, if no better entertainment were to be found — and he after enduring wounds and smarting to death. I can tell you a very different story about that place. A goat called Heiðrún stands up [on its hind-legs] in Valhalla biting the buds off the branches of that very famous tree which is called Læraŏ. From her teats runs the mead with which every day she fills a cauldron, which is so big that all the Einherjar can drink their fill from it.'

Gangleri said: 'What an exceedingly convenient goat for them. It must be a mighty good tree she feeds on!'

Then High One said: 'Still more remarkable is the hart Eikthyrnir, which stands in Valhalla devouring the branches of this tree. Such a huge stream comes from its horns that it falls down into Hvergelmir and thence flow the rivers called: Síŏ,[1] Víŏ,[2] Sekin, Ekin, Svöl,[3] Gunnthró,[4] Fjörm, Fimbulthul,[5] Gipul, Göpul,[6] Gömul,[7] Geirvimul.[8] These flow about the dwellings of

1 Slow.   4 Battle-defiant.   7 Old.
2 Broad.   5 Loud-bubbling.   8 Spear-teeming.
3 Cool.   6 Forward-rushing.

the gods. These are also mentioned: Thyn,[1] Vin, Thöll, Höll, Gráð,[2] Gunnthráin, Nyt, Naut, Nön,[3] Hrön, Vína,[4] Vegs-vin,[5] Thjóðnuma.'[6]

Then Gangleri remarked: 'This is wonderful news you are telling now. Valhalla must be an enormous house, and its doors must often be very crowded.'

Then High One answered: 'Why don't you ask how many doors the hall has, or how big they are? When you hear that you will say that it would be extraordinary if whoever wished could not go out and in; and in point of fact it is just as easy to find room inside as it is to enter it. You can hear this from the *Lay of Grímnir*:

> I think there are in Valhalla
> more than six hundred
> and forty doors;
> out of a single door at a time
> will tramp nine hundred and sixty men,
> champions advancing on the monster.'

Then Gangleri said: 'There is a great host in Valhalla, and, upon my word, Óðin is a very powerful chieftain to control so large an army. How do the Einherjar amuse themselves when they are not drinking?'

High One said: 'Every day after they have dressed, they put on their armour and go out into the courtyard and fight and lay one another low. That is their play and, when it is breakfast-time, they ride to the hall and sit down to drink, as it says here:

> All the champions
> every day
> contend in Óðin's courtyard;
> they choose the slain
> and ride from the field,
> thenceforth sit reconciled.

---

1 Frothing.   3 Strong.   5 Way-knowing.
2 Greedy.   4 Dwina.   6 Sweeping-people-away.

What you say, however, is true; Óðin is very powerful and there are many proofs of this. As is said here in the words of the Æsir themselves:

> The foremost of trees
> is the ash Yggdrasil,
> of ships Skíðblaðnir,
> of Æsir Óðin,
> Sleipnir of steeds,
> Bifröst of bridges,
> Bragi of poets,
> Hábrók of hawks
> and of hounds, Garm.'

Then Gangleri asked: 'Who owns the horse Sleipnir? What story is there about him?'

High One said: 'You don't know anything about Sleipnir, and you are ignorant of what led to his birth! Then that [story] will seem to you worth telling.

'In the early days of the settlement of the gods, when they had established Miðgarð and made Valhalla, there came a builder who offered to make them in eighteen months a stronghold so excellent that it would be safe and secure against cliff giants and frost ogres, even if they got inside Miðgarð. He stipulated this, however, as his reward: he was to have Freyja as his wife and possession of the sun and moon besides. Then the Æsir went into consultation and had a conference, and this bargain was struck with the builder, that he should become the owner of what he asked for, if he succeeded in building the stronghold in one winter; but if, on the first day of summer, any part of it was unfinished, he was to forfeit his reward; nor was he to receive anyone's help in the work. When they told him these terms, however, he asked them to let him have the help of his horse, which was called Svaðilfari, and Loki had his way when that was granted him.

'He began building the stronghold the first day of winter, and by night used his horse for hauling the stones for it. The Æsir were astonished at the size of the huge boulders the horse hauled, and it performed twice as much of that tremendous task as the builder. Now there were strong witnesses to their bargain and it was confirmed with many oaths, because the giant did not consider it safe to be among the Æsir without safe-conduct, if Thór should come home; at that time he had gone into the east to fight trolls. As winter drew to an end the building of the stronghold made good progress, and it was so high and strong that it could not be taken [by assault]. When it was three days to summer, the work had almost reached the gateway of the stronghold. The gods then sat down in their judgment seats and sought for a way out, asking one another who had given the advice to marry Freyja into Giantland, and so to ruin the sky and heaven as to take the sun and moon away and give them to the giants. They all agreed that the one who gives most bad counsels, Loki, Laufey's son, would have advised this, and they said he deserved an evil death if he did not devise a plan whereby the builder would lose his wages, and they laid [violent] hands on him. In his fright, however, Loki swore oaths that, no matter what it cost him, he would arrange things so that the builder should forfeit his wages. The same evening, when the builder was driving out after stones with the stallion Svaðilfari, a mare ran out of a wood up to the horse and whinnied to him. And when the stallion knew what kind of horse that was, it became frantic and broke its traces asunder and ran after the mare, but she took to the wood with the builder after her. He wanted to catch the stallion, but these horses galloped about all night and the work was delayed for that night. Next day not so much building had been done as before. Then, when the builder saw that the work would not be finished, he flew into a giant rage. When, however, the Æsir saw for certain that it was a giant who had come there, no reverence was shown for their oaths and they called on Thór. He came at once, and the next thing was that the hammer Mjöllnir was raised aloft. Thór paid the builder his wages, and it was not the sun and moon; he would not even allow him to live in Giantland, but struck him such a single blow that his skull shivered into fragments and he sent him down under Niflhel. Loki, however, had had such dealings with Svaðilfari that some time later he bore a foal. It was grey and had eight legs, and amongst gods and men that horse is the best. As it says in the *Sibyl's Vision*:

> Then all the Powers,
> gods most sacred,
> went to their judgment-seats,
> asked one another
> who had involved
> the air with evil,
> or conferred
> the bride of Óð
> on the ogre-kin.
>
> Oaths and words
> and vows were violated,
> all mighty speech
> that had passed between them.
> Thór alone struck there
> livid with anger,[1]
> seldom still he sits
> when he hears such things.'

Then Gangleri asked: 'What is there to tell about Skíðblaðnir, since it is the best of ships? Is there no ship as good or as big as it?'

High One replied: 'Skíðblaðnir is the best ship and built with the greatest skill, but Naglfar which is Muspell's is the biggest ship. Some dwarfs, the sons of Ívaldi, made Skíðblaðnir and gave the ship to Frey. It is so big that all the Æsir with weapons and armour can find room in it and, wherever it is going, a breeze springs up as soon as its sail is hoisted. Moreover, it is made of so many things and with such cunning that when it has not to go

---

1 Literally 'swollen with rage'.

to sea, it can be folded together like a cloth and kept in one's pouch.'

Then Gangleri remarked: 'Skíðblaðnir is a fine ship, and mighty magic will have been used to get it made like this. Now has Thór never had an experience in which he encountered something so strong in might and powerful in magic that it was too much for him?'

Then High One said: 'He has found many things hard to master but I doubt if anyone could tell you the stories and, even if something did overcome Thór on account of its magical power and strength, there is no need to tell the tale, since this happened more than once and yet everyone has to believe that Thór is exceedingly mighty.'

Then Gangleri said: 'It seems to me that I've asked you something no one is prepared to tell me about.'

Then Just-as-high said: 'Certain happenings have been reported to us that strike us as being incredible, but there is a man sitting nearby who will know the truth about them, and you may be sure, since he has never told a lie before, that he won't tell one for the first time now.'

Then Gangleri said: 'I'll stand here all ears for the answer to my question. On the other hand, if you can't tell me what I am asking, I maintain I've got the better of you.'

Then Third said: 'It is obvious that he wants to know this tale, although we don't think it a fine one to tell. You keep quiet.

'The beginning of the story is that Thór-the-charioteer was on a journey with his goats and in his chariot and with him the god Loki, when they came one evening to a farmer's where they got lodgings for the night. During the evening Thór took the goats and slaughtered them, then had them skinned and put into a cauldron. When they were cooked, Thór and his companion sat down to supper and Thór invited the farmer and his wife and children to the meal. The farmer's son was called Thjálfi and his daughter, Röskva. Thór spread the skins out away from the fire, and told the farmer and his household to throw the bones on to the skins. Thjálfi, the farmer's son, took firm hold of a thigh-bone of one of the goats and split it with his knife, breaking it for the marrow. Thór stayed there that night, and just before daybreak got up and dressed, took the hammer Mjöllnir, raised it and consecrated the goatskins. Then the goats stood up. One of them was lame of a hind leg; Thór noticed that and declared that the farmer and his household had done something silly with the bones; he knew that a thigh-bone was broken. There is no need to make a long story about it; everyone can guess how terrified the farmer would be when he saw Thór letting his eyebrows sink down over his eyes — but when he saw what he did of the eyes he thought he would drop down dead for the look in them alone. Thór gripped the handle of his hammer so that his knuckles went white. Then the farmer and his whole household did what you might expect, screamed out and begged for mercy for themselves, offering in compensation everything they possessed. But when Thór saw their terror, his anger left him and he calmed down and took from them in reconciliation their children Thjálfi and Röskva. They became his bondservants and accompanied him ever afterwards.

'He left his goats behind him there and set off on an expedition eastwards to Giantland, travelling all the way to the sea and then away over the deep ocean. When he came to land he went ashore and with him Loki and Thjálfi and Röskva. They had not walked very long before they came upon a big wood, and they walked the whole day till dark. Thjálfi, who could run faster than anyone else, was carrying Thór's knapsack, but they were not very well off for food.

'When it got dark they made a search for somewhere to stay the night, and came across an enormous hall with a door opening at the end as broad as the hall was wide. There they sought night quarters for themselves. But at midnight there was a great earthquake; the ground went rocking under them and the building shook. Thór stood up and called to his companions, and they made a search and discovered in the middle of the hall a side-room to the right, and went up to it. Thór sat down in the doorway, but the others went further in from him; they were terrified, but Thór gripped the handle of his hammer and determined to defend himself. Then they heard a great din of muffled roaring. When day came, Thór went outside and saw a man lying a short way off in the wood and he was no pygmy. He was asleep and snoring loudly. Thór thought he understood then what sort of noises they had been hearing in the night. He put on his belt of strength and his divine power increased, but at that moment the man woke up and sprang to his feet. And they say that for once Thór was too startled to hit him with the hammer, and asked him what his name was. The man replied it was Skrýmir;[1] "and there's no need for me to ask you yours", he said, "I know you are Ása-Thór. Have you moved my glove?" He stretched out his hand and picked up the glove. Then Thór realized that that was what he had had as a sleeping-hall in the night, and the side-room was the thumb.

'Skrýmir asked Thór if he would like to have his company and Thór said he would. Then Skrýmir undid his provision bag and got ready to eat breakfast, but Thór and his companions had theirs in another place. Skrýmir suggested that they should pool their provisions; Thór agreed to that, and Skrýmir tied up all their provisions in one bag and put it on his own back. He went on ahead during the day, taking immense strides, and late in the evening found them a lodging for the night under a large oak. Then Skrýmir told Thór he wished to lie down and go to sleep, "but you take the provision bag and get your supper ready". The next minute Skrýmir was asleep and snoring loudly. Thór took the provision bag intending to undo it, but, however incredible it may seem, it must be related that he was unable to get a single knot undone or strap-end moved so that it was tied

1 Big Fellow.

less tightly than before. When he saw he was wasting his time he grew angry, gripped the hammer Mjöllnir with both hands, stepped a pace forward to where Skrýmir was lying and struck him on the head. Skrýmir woke up and asked if a leaf had fallen on his head or if they had had supper and were ready for bed. Thór said they were just going to sleep, and they went under another oak tree. To tell you the truth they were much too frightened to sleep. At midnight Thór heard Skrýmir snoring so that the wood resounded. Then Thór got up, went to him, lifted his hammer quickly and fiercely and struck him in the middle of his crown; he knew that the face of the hammer sank deep into his head. At that instant Skrýmir woke up and asked: "What's the matter now? Did an acorn fall on my head? What's happened to you, Thór?" Thór, however, retreated hastily, saying he had just woken up and that it was the middle of the night and still time to sleep. He reflected, however, that if he got an opportunity of hitting him a third blow Skrýmir would never survive it, and he lay still, waiting for Skrýmir to fall asleep [again].

'A little before daybreak he knew from what he was hearing that Skrýmir had fallen asleep. He stood up and made for him, lifting the hammer with all his might and striking him on the temple that was turned up; the hammer sank in up to the handle. Skrýmir, however, sat up rubbing his cheek and asking: "Are there any birds up in the tree above me? When I was waking up I fancied that some droppings from the twigs fell on to my head. Are you awake, Thór? It's time to get up and dress. You haven't far to go now, however, to reach the stronghold called Útgarð. I've heard you whispering amongst yourselves that I'm no small man, but if you get to Útgarð you'll see bigger men there. Now I'm going to give you some good advice. Don't behave in an arrogant manner; Útgarð-Loki's retainers won't put up with the bragging of such whipper-snappers as you are. Your other course would be to go back and in my opinion it would be better for you to do that, but if you will go on, travel eastwards;

my way lies north to those mountains you will be able to see now."

'Skrýmir took the provision bag and throwing it over his back turned abruptly away from them into the wood. It is not related that the Æsir expressed any desire to meet him again.

'Thór and his companions continued their way and walked on till midday. Then they saw a stronghold on a plain. They had to bend their necks right back before they could see over the top of it. They went up to the stronghold and there was a gate in the entrance and it was shut. Thór went up to the gate but could not get it opened. Then they tried their hardest to get inside the stronghold and [finally] did so by squeezing between the bars of the gate. After that they saw a huge hall and went up to it. The door was open and, entering, they saw a large number of men and most of them pretty big, sitting on two benches. Next they came before the king, Útgarð-Loki, and greeted him, but it was some time before he took any notice of them. He smiled contemptuously at them and remarked: "News travels slowly from distant parts, or am I mistaken in thinking that this urchin is Thór-the-charioteer? You must be stronger than you look to me. At what arts do you and your companions think you excel? We don't allow anyone to stay with us who is not a past master of some craft or accomplishment."

'Then the one who brought up the rear, Loki, said: "I have an accomplishment which I am ready to try; there's no one here will eat faster than I can." Útgarð-Loki replied: "That's a feat if you can perform it and we'll put it to the test." He called over to the very end of the bench that the man called Logi should take the floor in front of the company and pit himself against Loki. Then a trencher was fetched and brought into the hall and filled with chopped-up meat. Loki sat down at one end and Logi at the other, and each of them ate as fast as he could. They met in the middle of the trencher and by then Loki had left only the bones of his meat, but Logi had eaten all his meat, bones, and trencher into the bargain, so everyone thought that Loki had lost the contest.

'Then Útgarð-Loki asked what the youngster there could do. Thjálfi said he would run a race against anyone Útgarð-Loki produced. Útgarð-Loki said that that was a good accomplishment; he reckoned he must be very good at running to perform this feat, yet he agreed it should be tried forthwith. Útgarð-Loki got up and went outside then, and there along a level bit of ground was a good running-track. Útgarð-Loki called to him a lad whose name was Hugi and told him to run a race with Thjálfi. They ran the first race and Hugi was so far ahead that he turned back to meet Thjálfi at the end of it.

'Then Útgarð-Loki said: "You will have to exert yourself a bit more, Thjálfi, if you are to win this contest and yet it's true that no men have [ever] come here who have struck me as being quicker on their feet than this." Then they ran the second race, and this time when Hugi came to the end and turned round, Thjálfi was a long cross-bow shot behind. Útgarð-Loki said: "I think Thjálfi is a good runner, but I don't believe he will win the contest now; we'll prove it, however, when they run the third race." Then they ran yet another race. Hugi had reached the end and turned back, however, before Thjálfi had come halfway and everyone said that this sport had been put to the test.

'Then Útgarð-Loki asked Thór what accomplishment it would be he was going to display to them — and men after telling such great tales of his mighty deeds. Thór answered that he would like best to pit himself against someone in drinking. Útgarð-Loki said that that might well be and went into the hall and calling his cup-bearer bade him fetch the sconce-horn the retainers were accustomed to drink from. The cup-bearer at once came forward with the horn and placed it in Thór's hands. Útgarð-Loki remarked: "We consider it good drinking if this horn is drained at one drink, some men take two to empty it, but no one is such a wretched drinker that he can't finish it in three." Thór looked at the horn. It did not strike him as being very big, although it was a bit on the long side, and he was very thirsty. He began drinking in great gulps and thought he would not need to bend to the horn more than once. When, however, his breath failed and he raised his head from it to see what progress had been made in the drinking, it seemed to him that it was only a little lower in the horn than before.

'Then Útgarð-Loki said: "You drank well but not too much; I would never have believed it if I had been told that Ása-Thór couldn't take a bigger drink. However, I know you will empty it at the second draught." Thór made no reply, put the horn to his mouth intending to take a bigger drink and strove at the drinking until he was out of breath; yet he saw that the end of the horn would not tilt up as much as he would have liked. When he took the horn from his mouth and looked into it, it seemed to him that he had made still less impression than before, although there was now enough space between the rim and the liquor to carry the horn without spilling.

'Then Útgarð-Loki said: "What about it, Thór? Aren't you leaving more for the one drink left over than will be quite convenient for you? It seems to me, if you are going to empty the horn at the third draught, that this will have to be the biggest. You won't be considered so great a man here amongst us as you are with the Æsir, you know, unless you can give a better account of yourself in other contests than it seems to me you will in this." At that Thór grew angry, put the horn to his mouth and took a tremendously long drink as hard as he could; and when he looked at the horn, he had at any rate made a slight difference. He then gave up the horn and would drink no more.

'Útgarð-Loki remarked: "It is evident that your strength is not as great as we had imagined. But do you want to make trial of any other feats? It is clear that you don't show to advantage in this one." Thór answered: "I can make trial of some feats yet; when I was at home with the Æsir, however, I'd have thought it strange for drinks like these to be called little — what sport are you proposing for me now?"

'Then Útgarð-Loki said: "Youngsters here perform the feat — it's not thought much of — of lifting my cat up from the ground; I would never have suggested such a thing to Ása-Thór if I'd not seen that you aren't nearly as strong as I thought you were." Thereupon a grey cat jumped forward on to the hall floor. It was rather a big one, but Thór went up to it, put his arm round under the middle of its belly, and lifted up. The cat arched its back as Thór raised his arm, and when he was stretching up as high as he could, the cat had to lift one of its paws [from the floor]; that was all Thór could do in that trial of skill.

'Then Útgarð-Loki said: "This contest has gone as I expected; it's rather a big cat and Thór is a short little fellow compared with such big men as we have here." At that Thór said: "Call me little if you like, but let someone come and wrestle with me now; now I am angry!" Útgarð-Loki looked along the bench and said: "I don't see anyone here who wouldn't feel it beneath him to wrestle with you." He added, however, "Wait a bit, call my foster-mother, the old woman Elli, here, and let Thór wrestle with her if he wants to. She has brought down men who have struck me as being stronger-looking than Thór."

'Thereupon an aged crone came into the hall and Útgarð-Loki said she was to come to grips with Ása-Thór. There is no need to make a long story of it. The wrestling went so that the harder Thór exerted himself the firmer she stood her ground. Then the old woman began trying holds and Thór lost his balance; there was a tremendous tussle, but it was not long before Thór fell on to one knee. Útgarð-Loki went up to them then and told them to stop wrestling, saying there was no need for Thór to offer to wrestle with any more of his retainers. By that time it was late in the evening. Útgarð-Loki showed Thór and his companions where to sit down and they stayed there the night and were shown great hospitality.

'As soon as dawn broke the next day Thór and his companions got up, dressed, and were ready to go away. Then Útgarð-Loki came to where they were and had a table set up for them. There was no lack of good cheer in the way of food and drink. When they had finished the meal, they set out on their journey and Útgarð-Loki accompanied them, going out of the stronghold with them. At their parting he addressed Thór, asking him how he thought his journey had turned out and whether he had ever met a man mightier than he [Útgarð-Loki] was. Thór replied that he would not deny that he had been put to shame in their dealings with each other, "I know besides that you'll dub me a nobody and I don't like that."

'Then Útgarð-Loki said: "I'm going to tell you the truth now that you've come out of the stronghold — if I live and have any say in the matter, you are never going to come inside it again; upon my word you'd never have got in if I'd known you had so much strength; you nearly landed us in disaster. But I have deceived you with spells. The first time when I came across you in the wood I'd come to meet you, and when you were to undo the provision bag, I'd tied it up with iron wire and you didn't discover where to undo it. After that you hit me three blows with the hammer, the first of these was the least and yet if it had reached me it would have been my death. Where you saw a saddle-backed hill close to my stronghold and in it three square-shaped valleys and one very deep — they were the marks left by your hammer. I put the saddle-backed hill in front of your blows, but you didn't see that. The same thing goes for the contests in which you strove against my retainers. The first was what Loki did. He was very hungry and ate fast, but the man called Logi was "wildfire" and he burned the trencher as quickly as he did the chopped meat. And when Thjálfi was running against the one called Hugi, that was my thought, and Thjálfi couldn't be expected to compete in speed with that. And when you were drinking from the horn and thought you were being slow, upon my word, I never would have believed such a miracle possible; the other end of the horn was in the sea but you didn't perceive that, and now when you come to the ocean you'll see how much you have made it shrink." That is called the ebb-tide now. He continued: "I thought it no less wonderful when you lifted up the cat and, to tell you the truth, everyone who saw it was terrified when you lifted one of its paws from the ground. That cat was not what it appeared to be; it was the Miðgarð Serpent that lies curled round the world and is scarcely long enough head to tail to encircle the earth. You stretched up so high that it wasn't far to the sky. It was a marvellous thing, too, that you held out so long in the wrestling match and only fell down on to one knee when you were struggling with Elli, because there never has been, nor ever will be anyone (if he grows old enough to become aged), who is not tripped up by old age. And now, as a matter of fact, we are going to part and it will be better for us both for you not to come to see me again. I shall go on defending my stronghold with some such magic or other so that you will not win any power over me."

'When Thór heard this speech he gripped his hammer and swung it aloft but, when he was going to strike, he saw no Útgarð-Loki. Then he turned round to the stronghold with the idea of destroying it. He saw no stronghold there — [only] spacious and beautiful plains. He turned away and went on his journey until he came back to Thrúðvangar. To tell you the truth, however, it was then he resolved to see if he could contrive an encounter with the Miðgarð Serpent, as he afterwards did. Now I don't think that anyone could tell you a better tale about this expedition of Thór's.'

Then Gangleri said: 'Útgarð-Loki is very powerful but he makes much use of guile and magic. Still, the fact that his retainers were so strong shows how powerful he is. Did Thór not take vengeance for this?'

High One answered: 'One doesn't need to be an authority to

know that Thór made amends for the expedition which has just
been described; he did not stay long at home before he got ready
for a journey in such haste that he took with him neither chariot
nor goats nor companions. He went out of Ásgarð disguised as a
youth and came in the evening to a giant called Hymir. Thór
stayed there that night, and at daybreak Hymir got up and
dressed and prepared to go sea-fishing in a rowing-boat. Thór
sprang up and was soon ready and asking Hymir to let him go
rowing with him. Hymir said that he would not be much help,
as he was such a scrap of a young fellow: "You'll catch cold if I
sit as long and as far out to sea as I usually do." Thór, however,
said he would be able to row a long way out from the shore all
the same, and that it wasn't certain that he would be the first to
demand to be rowed back; and he got so angry with the giant
that he was ready incontinently to set the hammer ringing on his
head. He controlled himself, however, as he was intending to try
his strength in another place. He asked Hymir what they were to
take as bait, but Hymir told him to get his own. Then Thór
turned away to where he saw a herd of oxen belonging to Hymir
and taking the biggest ox, which was called Sky-bellower, he
struck off its head and went down to the sea with it. By then
Hymir had launched his boat. Thór went on board and sitting
down in the stern took two oars and rowed. Hymir thought they
made rapid progress from his rowing.

'Hymir rowed bow and the rowing went on apace until
Hymir said that now he had come to those banks where he was
accustomed to sit and catch flat fish, but Thór said he wanted to
row much farther out and they had another bout of fast rowing.
Then Hymir said that they had come so far out that it would be
dangerous to sit there on account of the Miðgarð Serpent. Thór,
however, declared his intention of rowing for a bit yet, and did
so, and Hymir was not at all pleased at that.

'When Thór shipped his oars, he made ready a very strong line
and the hook was just as big and firm; baiting the hook with the

ox-head he flung it overboard. It sank to the bottom, and it's a fact that, on this occasion, Thór made as great a fool of the Miðgarð Serpent as Útgarð-Loki had of Thór when he was trying to lift the serpent up with his arm. The Miðgarð Serpent snapped at the ox-head, but the hook stuck fast in the roof of its mouth and, when it realized that, it jerked away so hard that both Thór's fists knocked against the gunwale. Then Thór grew angry and, exerting [all] his divine strength, dug in his heels so hard that both legs went through the boat and he was digging his heels in on the sea bottom. He drew the serpent up on board, and it must be said that no one has seen anything to be afraid of who didn't see how Thór fixed the serpent with his eye and how the serpent glared back, belching poison.

'We are told that the giant Hymir lost colour then, and turned pale with fear when he saw the serpent and the sea tumbling in and out of the vessel too. The very moment Thór gripped his hammer and raised it aloft, the giant fumbled for his bait-knife and cut Thór's line off at the gunwale, and the serpent sank back into the sea. Thór flung his hammer after it and people say that this struck its head off in the waves; but I think the truth is that the Miðgarð Serpent is still alive and is lying in the ocean. Thór clenched his fist and gave Hymir a box on the ear so that he fell overboard head first, but he himself waded ashore.'

Then Gangleri asked: 'Are there any more remarkable stories about the Æsir? Thór performed a very mighty deed on this journey.'

High One replied: 'I will tell you about something that seemed far more important to the Æsir. The beginning of this story is that Baldr the Good had some terrible dreams that threatened his life. When he told the Æsir these dreams, they took counsel together and it was decided to seek protection for Baldr from every kind of peril. Frigg exacted an oath from fire and water, iron and all kinds of metals, stones, earth, trees, ailments, beasts, birds, poison and serpents, that they would not harm Baldr. And when this had been done and put to the test, Baldr and the Æsir used to amuse themselves by making him stand up at their assemblies for some of them to throw darts at, others to strike and the rest to throw stones at. No matter what was done he was never hurt, and everyone thought that a fine thing. When Loki, Laufey's son, saw that, however, he was annoyed that Baldr was not hurt and he went disguised as a woman to Fensalir to visit Frigg. Frigg asked this woman if she knew what the Æsir were doing at the assembly. She answered that they were all throwing things at Baldr, moreover that he was not being hurt. Frigg remarked: "Neither weapons nor trees will injure Baldr; I have taken an oath from them all." The woman asked: "Has everything sworn you an oath to spare Baldr?" Frigg replied: "West of Valhalla grows a little bush called mistletoe, I did not exact an oath from it; I thought it too young." Thereupon the woman disappeared.

'Loki took hold of the mistletoe, pulled it up and went to the assembly. Now Höð was standing on the outer edge of the circle of men because he was blind. Loki asked him: "Why aren't you throwing darts at Baldr?" He replied: "Because I can't see where Baldr is, and, another thing, I have no weapon." Then Loki said: "You go and do as the others are doing and show Baldr honour like other men. I will show you where he is standing: throw this twig at him." Höð took the mistletoe and aimed at Baldr as directed by Loki. The dart went right through him and he fell dead to the ground. This was the greatest misfortune ever to befall gods and men.

'When Baldr had fallen, the Æsir were struck dumb and not one of them could move a finger to lift him up; each looked at the other, and all were of one mind about the perpetrator of that deed, but no one could take vengeance; the sanctuary there was so holy. When the Æsir did try to speak, weeping came first, so that no one could tell the other his grief in words. Óðin, however, was the most affected by this disaster, since he understood best what a loss and bereavement the death of Baldr was for the Æsir. When the gods had recovered from the first shock Frigg spoke. She asked which of the Æsir wished to win her whole affection and favour. Would he ride the road to Hel to try if he could find Baldr, and offer Hel a ransom if she would allow Baldr to come home to Ásgarð? The one who undertook this journey was a son of Óðin called Hermóð the Bold. Then they caught Óðin's horse, Sleipnir, and led him forward, and Hermóð mounted that steed and galloped away.

'The Æsir, however, took Baldr's body and carried it down to the sea. Baldr's ship was called Ringhorn,[1] it was a very large ship. The gods wanted to launch it and to build Baldr's funeral pyre on it, but they could not move it at all. They sent to Giantland then for the ogress called Hyrrokkin. And when she came — she was riding a wolf with vipers for reins — she jumped off her steed and Óðin called to four berserks to guard it, but they were unable to hold it fast till they struck it down. Then Hyrrokkin went to the prow of the vessel and at the first shove launched it in such a way that the rollers burst into flame and the whole world trembled. Thór became angry then and seizing his hammer would have cracked her skull had not all the gods begged protection for her.

'Then Baldr's body was carried out on to the ship, and when his wife Nanna, daughter of Nep, saw that, her heart broke from grief and she died. She was carried on to the pyre and it was set alight. Thór was standing by and consecrating it with Mjöllnir, when a dwarf called Lit ran in front of his feet. Thór tripped him up and kicked him into the fire, and he was burned to death. All sorts of people came to this cremation. First and foremost, Óðin, accompanied by Frigg and his valkyries and ravens. Frey drove in a chariot drawn by the boar called Gold-bristle or Razor-tooth. Heimdall rode the horse called Gold-tuft and Freyja was driving her cats. A great crowd of frost ogres and cliff giants came too.

1 Curved-prow.

Óðin laid on the pyre the gold ring which is called Draupnir; it had this characteristic afterwards, that every ninth night there dropped from it eight rings of equal value. Baldr's horse with all its harness was led to the pyre.

'Concerning Hermóð, however, there is this to tell. For nine nights he rode dales so deep and dark that he saw nothing, until he reached the river Gjöll and rode over its bridge; it is thatched with gleaming gold. The maiden who guards that bridge is called Móðguð. She asked him his name and family and said that the day before five troops of dead men had ridden over the bridge, "but the bridge resounds as much under you alone, and you don't look like a man who has died. Why are you riding here on the road to Hel?" He replied: "I must ride to Hel to seek for Baldr. Have you seen anything of him on his way there?" She said that Baldr had ridden past over the bridge of the Gjöll, "but the road to Hel lies downwards and northwards".

'Hermóð rode on then till he came to the gates of Hel. Then he alighted and tightened his stirrups, remounted, and dug in his spurs, and the horse jumped over the gate with such vigour that it came nowhere near it. Then Hermóð rode right up to the hall and dismounted. He went inside and saw his brother Baldr sitting on the high seat there. Hermóð stayed there that night. In the morning he asked Hel if Baldr might ride home with him, telling her how much the gods were weeping. Hel said, however, that this test should be made as to whether Baldr was loved as much as people said. "If everything in the world, both dead or alive, weeps for him, then he shall go back to the Æsir, but he shall remain with Hel if anyone objects or will not weep." Then Hermóð stood up and Baldr led him out of the hall and taking [off] the ring Draupnir sent it to Óðin in remembrance, but Nanna sent Frigg, along with other gifts, linen [for a head-dress], and Fulla a gold ring. Hermóð rode back again to Ásgarð and [when] he arrived [there] related all he had seen and heard.

'Thereupon the Æsir sent messengers throughout the whole

world to ask for Baldr to be wept out of Hel; and everything did that — men and beasts, and the earth, and the stones and trees and all metals — just as you will have seen these things weeping when they come out of frost and into the warmth. When the messengers were coming home, having made a good job of their errand, they met with a giantess sitting in a cave; she gave her name as Thökk. They asked her to weep Baldr out of Hel. She answered:

> Thökk will weep
> dry tears
> at Baldr's embarkation;
> the old fellow's son
> was no use to me
> alive or dead,
> let Hel hold what she has.

It is thought that the giantess there was Loki, Laufey's son — who has done most harm amongst the Æsir.'

Then Gangleri said: 'Loki has a great deal to answer for, since first he caused Baldr to be killed, and then prevented him from being freed from Hel. Was any vengeance taken on him for this?'

High One said: 'This was requited him in a manner he will long remember. When the gods had become as wrathful with him as might be expected, he ran away and hid himself on a mountain. There he built himself a house with four doors so that he could see out of it in all directions. Often during the day, however, he changed himself into the shape of a salmon and hid in the place called the waterfall of Fránang. He tried to anticipate in his mind what contraption the Æsir would use to catch him in the waterfall so, [once] when he was sitting indoors over a fire, he took linen twine and twisted it into meshes in the way that nets have been made since. Then he saw that the Æsir were almost on him — Óðin had seen where he was from Hliðskjálf — so throwing the net on to the fire, he jumped up and out into the river.

'When the Æsir arrived, the one who went into the house first was the wisest of them all — his name was Kvasir. When he saw in the fire the white ash to which the net had burned, he understood that that was a contraption for catching fish and said so to the Æsir. Thereupon they made a net in imitation of the one they could see from the burned-out ashes Loki had made. When the net was ready, the Æsir went to the river and cast it into the waterfall. Thór was holding on to one end of the net and the rest of the Æsir the other as they dragged it. Loki, however, got ahead and lay down between two stones. They dragged the net over him and, realizing that there was something alive there, went up the waterfall a second time and flung the net out, weighting it so heavily that nothing could pass under it. Loki swam ahead of the net then but, when he saw the sea was close to, he jumped back over its edge-rope and hurried up into the waterfall. This time the gods saw where he had gone; they went back again to the waterfall and dividing their forces into two groups, while Thór waded in mid-stream, they made for the [open] sea. Then Loki saw that he had only two means of escape, either to risk his life by jumping out to sea or to try once more to leap over the net. He chose the latter, jumping as quickly as possible over its edge-rope. Thór clutched at him and caught him, but he slipped through his hand until he had him fast by the tail, and it is for this reason that the salmon tapers towards the tail.

'After that Loki was taken unconditionally and put into a cave. Taking three flat stones, the gods set them up on end and bored a hole through each. Then Loki's sons were captured, Vali and Nari or Narfi. The Æsir changed Vali into a wolf and he tore asunder his brother Narfi. The Æsir took his entrails and with them bound Loki over the edges of the three stones — one under his shoulder, the second under his loins, the third under his knee-joints — and these bonds became iron. Then Skaði took a poisonous snake and fastened it up over him so that the venom from it should drop on to his face. His wife Sigyn, however, sits by him holding a basin under the poison drops. When the basin becomes full she goes away to empty it, but in the meantime the venom drips on to his face and then he shudders so violently that the whole earth shakes — you call that an earthquake. There he will lie in bonds until Ragnarök.'[1]

Then Gangleri said: 'What is there to relate about Ragnarök? I have never heard tell of this before.'

High One said: 'There are many and great tidings to tell about it. First will come the winter called Fimbulvetr.[2] Snow will drive from all quarters, there will be hard frosts and biting winds; the sun will be no use. There will be three such winters on end with no summer between. Before that, however, three other winters will pass accompanied by great wars throughout the whole world. Brothers will kill each other for the sake of gain, and no one will spare father or son in manslaughter or in incest. As it says in the *Sibyl's Vision*:

> Brothers will fight
> and kill each other,
> siblings
> do incest;
> men will know misery,
> adulteries be multiplied,
> an axe-age, a sword-age,
> shields will be cloven,
> a wind-age, a wolf-age,
> before the world's ruin.

'Then will occur what will seem a great piece of news, the wolf will swallow the sun and that will seem a great disaster to men. Then another wolf will seize the moon and that one too will do great harm. The stars will disappear from heaven. Then this will come to pass, the whole surface of the earth and the mountains will tremble so [violently] that trees will be uprooted from the ground, mountains will crash down, and all fetters and bonds will be snapped and severed. The wolf Fenrir will get loose then. The sea will lash against the land because the Miðgarð Serpent

1 The Twilight of the Gods.   2 Terrible Winter.

is writhing in giant fury trying to come ashore. At that time, too, the ship known as Naglfar will become free. It is made of dead men's nails, so it is worth warning you that, if anyone dies with his nails uncut, he will greatly increase the material for that ship which both gods and men devoutly hope will take a long time building. In this tidal wave, however, Naglfar will be launched. The name of the giant steering Naglfar is Hrym. The wolf Fenrir will advance with wide open mouth, his upper jaw against the sky, his lower on the earth (he would gape more widely still if there were room) and his eyes and nostrils will blaze with fire. The Miðgarð Serpent will blow so much poison that the whole sky and sea will be spattered with it; he is most terrible and will be on the other side of the wolf.

'In this din the sky will be rent asunder and the sons of Muspell ride forth from it. Surt will ride first and with him fire blazing both before and behind. He has a very good sword and it shines more brightly than the sun. When they ride over Bifröst, how-ever — as has been said before — that bridge will break. The sons of Muspell will push forward to the plain called Vígríð and the wolf Fenrir and the Miðgarð Serpent will go there too. Loki and Hrym with all the frost giants will also be there by then, and all the family of Hel will accompany Loki. The sons of Muspell, however, will form a host in themselves and that a very bright one. The plain Vígríð is a hundred and twenty leagues in every direction.

'When these things are happening, Heimdall will stand up and blow a great blast on the horn Gjöll and awaken all the gods and they will hold an assembly. Then Óðin will ride to Mímir's spring and ask Mímir's advice for himself and his company. The ash Yggdrasil will tremble and nothing in heaven or earth will be free from fear. The Æsir and all the Einherjar will arm them-selves and press forward on to the plain. Óðin will ride first in a helmet of gold and a beautiful coat of mail and with his spear Gungnir, and he will make for the wolf Fenrir. Thór will advance at his side but will be unable to help him, because he will have his hands full fighting the Miðgarð Serpent. Frey will fight against Surt and it will be a hard conflict before Frey falls; the loss of the good sword that he gave to Skírnir will bring about his death. Then the hound Garm, which was bound in front of Gnipahellir,[1] will also get free; he is the worst sort of monster. He will battle with Týr and each will kill the other. Thór will slay the Miðgarð Serpent but stagger back only nine paces before he falls down dead, on account of the poison blown on him by the serpent. The wolf will swallow Óðin and that will be his death. Immediately afterwards, however, Víðar will stride forward and place one foot on the lower jaw of the wolf. On this foot he will be wearing the shoe which has been in the making since the beginning of time; it consists of the strips of leather men pare off at the toes and heels of their shoes, and for this reason people who want to help the Æsir must throw away these strips. Víðar will take the wolf's upper jaw in one hand and tear his throat asunder and that will be the wolf's death. Loki will battle with Heimdall and each will kill the other. Thereupon Surt will fling fire over the earth and burn up the whole world. As it says in the *Sibyl's Vision*:

> Heimdall blows loud
> his horn raised aloft,
> Óðin speaks
> with Mímir's head;
> Yggdrasil trembles,
> old outspreading ash,
> and groans
> as the giant gets free.
>
> How fare the Æsir?
> How fare the elves?
> All Giantland resounds —
> the Æsir in assembly;
> inhabitants of hillsides groan
> dwarfs
> by their doorways of stone.
> Do you know any more or not?

1 Cliff-cave leading to Hel.

Hrym drives from the east
holds high his shield before him,
Jörmungand writhes
in giant rage;
the serpent churns up waves;
screaming for joy
ghastly eagle will tear
dead bodies with his beak.

From the east sails a ship,
from the sea will come
the people of Muspell
with Loki as pilot;
all sons of fiends
are rowing with Fenrir,
with them on this voyage
is Býleist's brother. [1]

Surt from the south
comes with spoiler-of-twigs [2]
blazing his sword
[like] sun of the Mighty Ones;
mountains will crash down,
troll-women stumble,
men tread the road to Hel,
heaven's rent asunder.

Then occurs
Hlín's second grief,
when Óðin goes
to fight the wolf
and Beli's bane [3]
turns, fair, on Surt,
then will Frigg's
beloved die.

To fight the wolf
goes Óðin's son,
Víðar
is on his way;

1 Loki.　　　　2 Fire.　　　　3 Frey.

> sword in hand
> he will pierce the heart
> of Hveðrung's son.
> Thus is his sire avenged.
>
> The famous son
> of Earth falls back,
> fainting from the serpent
> fearing not attack.
> All mankind
> must abandon home
> when Miðgarð's Buckler[1]
> strikes in wrath.
>
> The sun will go black
> earth sink in the sea,
> heaven be stripped
> of its bright stars;
> smoke rage
> and fire,
> leaping the flame
> lick heaven itself.

Further it says here:

> Vígríð's the plain
> where the conflict takes place
> between Surt and the kindly gods.
> One hundred and twenty
> leagues each way
> is the plain for them appointed.'

Then Gangleri asked: 'What will happen afterwards, when heaven and earth and the whole world has been burned and all the gods are dead and all the Einherjar and the whole race of man? Didn't you say before that everyone will go on living for ever in some world or other?'

Then Third answered: 'There will be many good dwelling-places then and many bad. The best place to be in at that time

1 Thór.

will be Gimlé in heaven, and for those that like it there is plenty of good drink in the hall called Brimir that is on Ókolnir.[1] There is also an excellent hall on Niðafjöll[2] called Sindri; it is made of red gold. Good and righteous men will live in these halls. On Nástrandir[3] there is a large and horrible hall whose doors face north; it is made of the backs of serpents woven together like wattle-work, with all their heads turning in to the house and spewing poison so that rivers of it run through the hall. Perjurers and murderers wade these rivers as it says here:

> I know a hall
> whose doors face north
> on Nástrand
> far from the sun,
> poison drips
> from lights in the roof;
> that building is woven
> of backs of snakes.
> There heavy streams
> must be waded through
> by breakers of pledges
> and murderers.

But it is worst [of all] in Hvergelmir.

> There Niðhogg bedevils
> the bodies of the dead.'

Then Gangleri asked: 'Will any of the gods be living then? Will there be any earth or heaven then?'

High One said: 'At that time earth will rise out of the sea and be green and fair, and fields of corn will grow that were never sown. Víðar and Váli will be living, so neither the sea nor Surt's Fire will have done them injury, and they will inhabit Iðavöll where Ásgarð used to be. And the sons of Thór, Móði and Magni will come there and possess Mjöllnir. After that Baldr and Höð will come from Hel. They will all sit down

1 Never Cold.   2 Dark Mountains.   3 Corpse-strands.

together and converse, calling to mind their hidden lore and talking about things that happened in the past, about the Miðgarð Serpent and the wolf Fenrir. Then they will find there in the grass the golden chessmen the Æsir used to own. As it is said:

> Víðar and Váli
> when Surt's fire has died
> will dwell in the temples,
> Móði and Magni
> Thór's Mjöllnir will own
> at the end of the battle.

While the world is being burned by Surt, in a place called Hoddmímir's Wood, will be concealed two human beings called Líf and Lífthrasir. Their food will be the morning dews, and from these men will come so great a stock that the whole world will be peopled, as it says here:

> Líf and Lífthrasir
> in Hoddmímir's wood
> will be hidden;
> the morning dews
> their food and drink
> from thence will come men after men.

And you will think this strange, but the sun will have borne a daughter no less lovely than herself, and she will follow the paths of her mother, as it says here:

> Glory-of-elves[1] to a girl
> will give birth
> before Fenrir overtakes her,
> when the gods are dead
> she will pursue
> the paths of her mother.

And now, if you have anything more to ask, I can't think how you can manage it, for I've never heard anyone tell more of the story of the world. Make what use of it you can.'

1 The sun.

The next thing was that Gangleri heard a tremendous noise on all sides and turned about; and when he had looked all round him [he found] that he was standing in the open air on a level plain. He saw neither hall nor stronghold. Then he went on his way and coming home to his kingdom related the tidings he had seen and heard, and after him these stories have been handed down from one man to another.

SELECTIONS FROM
POETIC DICTION

SELECTIONS FROM
POETIC DICTION

There was a man called Ægir or Hlér, who lived on the island now known as Hlésey.[1] He was very skilled in magic. He went on an expedition to Ásgarð to visit the Æsir, who foresaw his journey and made him welcome, although they also worked a good many spells for him. When drinking-time in the evening came round, Óðin had swords brought into the hall and they were so bright that they illumined it, and no other lights were used while the drinking went on. Then the Æsir held festival, and twelve, that is those Æsir who had to be judges, sat down in their high seats. Their names are as follows: Thór, Njörð, Frey, Týr, Heimdall, Bragi, Víðar, Váli, Ull, Hœnir, Forseti, Loki; the goddesses who did likewise were Frigg, Freyja, Gefjon, Iðun, Gerð, Sigyn, Fulla, Nanna. Everything he saw there seemed splendidly lavish to Ægir. All the panelling was covered with fine shields. Moreover the mead was heady and a great deal of it was drunk. Bragi sat next Ægir and they occupied themselves in drinking and exchanging stories. Bragi told Ægir many tales about the doings of the gods.

He began relating how once three Æsir, Óðin, Loki and Hœnir, had left home and travelled over mountains and desert places without any provisions. Coming down into a valley they saw a herd of oxen and took one and set about cooking it. When they thought it was ready and scattered the fire, it was not done.

1 Læsö.

Some time later when they scattered the fire for a second time and it was [still] uncooked, they began to discuss amongst themselves what could be the cause. Then they heard a voice from an oak tree above them say that what was sitting up there was preventing their meat from being done. They looked up and saw an eagle sitting there, and it wasn't a small one.

The eagle said: 'If you give me my fill of the ox, then your meat will get done.' They agreed to this. Then it sailed down from the tree and settling on the meat snatched up at once, without any hesitation, two of the thighs and both the shoulders of the ox. At that Loki grew angry and catching up a great stick and thrusting with all his might he drove it into the eagle's body. The eagle recoiled from the blow and flew up into the air with one end of the stick stuck firmly in its back and Loki clinging to the other. The eagle was flying only just high enough for Loki's feet to be dragging along stones and scree and bushes, and he thought his arms would be pulled from their sockets. He called out imploring the eagle for mercy but it replied that it would not let Loki go unless he swore an oath to bring it Iðun and her apples out of Ásgarð. Loki was willing so he was released and went back to his companions, and no more is told of their journey on this occasion until they came home.

At the time agreed on, Loki enticed Iðun out from Ásgarð into a wood, telling her that he had found some apples she would prize greatly and asking her to bring her own with her for comparison. Then the giant Thjazi came there in the form of an eagle, and seizing Iðun flew away with her to his house in Thrymheim.

The Æsir, however, were much dismayed at Iðun's disappearance, and they soon grew old and grey-haired. They held an assembly and asked one another when Iðun had last been heard of, and realized that the last time she had been seen she was going out of Ásgarð with Loki. Then Loki was captured and brought to the assembly and threatened with death or torture. He grew so frightened that he said he would go after Iðun into Giantland, if Freyja would lend him her falcon coat. When he got the falcon coat, he flew north to Giantland. Loki arrived at the giant Thjazi's on a day when he had gone out rowing on the sea and Iðun was at home alone. Loki changed her into the form of a nut, and holding her in his claws flew off at top speed. When Thjazi came home, however, and saw that Iðun was missing, he assumed the shape of an eagle and flew after Loki, with a tremendous rush of air in his wake. The Æsir, seeing the falcon flying with the nut and the eagle in pursuit, went out under the walls of Ásgarð carrying bundles of plane shavings. When the falcon reached the stronghold, he dropped plumb down at the fortress wall and then the Æsir set fire to the plane shavings. The eagle, however, was unable to check his course when he lost the falcon and his feathers caught fire and then he did stop. The Æsir were hard by then and they killed the giant Thjazi inside the gates, and that slaying is very famous.

Now giant Thjazi's daughter Skaði took helmet, coat-of-mail and a complete outfit of weapons and went to Ásgarð to avenge her father. The Æsir, however, offered her compensation and damages, and first that she should choose a husband from amongst the Æsir and choose him by his feet without seeing any more of him. Then she saw a very beautiful pair of feet and said: 'I choose this one; there's not much that's ugly about Baldr!' — but that was Njörð of Nóatún.

A further condition was that the Æsir should make her laugh — which she thought would be impossible. When Loki, however, by his tricks succeeded in doing this their reconciliation was complete.

We are told that Óðin [further] compensated her by taking Thjazi's eyes and throwing them up into the sky, making of them two stars.

Then Ægir said: 'It seems to me that Thjazi was very powerful. What family did he come from?'

Bragi replied: 'His father was called Ölvaldi and you would find it interesting if I told you about him. He possessed a great deal of gold and when he died and his sons were going to divide the inheritance, they allotted the gold they were sharing between them in this way: each was to take the same-sized mouthfuls of it. Thjazi was one of them, Iði the second, and Gang the third. So now we have the expression by which we call gold the mouthful of these giants, and we conceal it in runes or poetry by calling it their speech or words or reckoning.'

Ægir asked again: 'Where did the accomplishment known as poetry come from?'

Bragi answered: 'The beginning of it was that the gods were at war with the people known as the Vanir and they arranged for a peace-meeting between them and made a truce in this way: they both went up to a crock and spat into it. When they were going away, the gods took the truce token and would not allow it to be lost, and made of it a man. He was called Kvasir. He is so wise that nobody asks him any question he is unable to answer. He travelled far and wide over the world to teach men wisdom and came once to feast with some dwarfs, Fjalar and Galar. These called him aside for a word in private and killed him, letting his blood run into two crocks and one kettle. The kettle was called Óðrörir, but the crocks were known as Són and Boðn. They mixed his blood with honey, and it became the mead which makes whoever drinks of it a poet or scholar. The dwarfs told the Æsir that Kvasir had choked with learning, because there was no one sufficiently well-informed to compete with him in know-ledge.

'Then the dwarfs invited a giant called Gilling to their home with his wife, and they asked him to go out rowing on the sea with them. When they were far out, however, the dwarfs rowed on to a rock and upset the boat. Gilling could not swim and was drowned, but the dwarfs righted their craft and rowed ashore. They told his wife about this accident and she was very distressed and wept aloud. Fjalar asked her if she would be easier in her mind about it if she looked out to sea in the direction of where he had been drowned. She wanted to do this. Then he spoke with his brother Galar, telling him to climb up above the door when she was going out and let a millstone fall on to her head; he said he was tired of her wailing. Galar did so. When Gilling's son, Suttung, heard of this, he went to the dwarfs and seized them and took them out to sea and put them on to a skerry covered by the tide. They begged Suttung to spare their lives offering him as compensation for his father the precious mead, and that brought about their reconciliation. Suttung took the mead home and hid it in a place called Hnitbjörg and he appointed his daughter Gunnlöð as its guardian.

'This is why we call poetry Kvasir's blood, or dwarfs' drink or intoxication, or some sort of liquid of Óðrörir or Boðn or Són, or dwarfs' ship, because it was that mead which ransomed them from death on the skerry, or Suttung's mead or Hnitbjörg's sea.'

Then Ægir spoke: 'It seems to me that to call poetry by these names obscures things. How did the Æsir acquire Suttung's mead?'

Bragi answered: 'The story goes that Óðin left home once and came across nine serfs mowing hay. He asked if they would like him to sharpen their scythes and they said they would. So he took a hone from his belt and put an edge on their tools and they all thought they cut much better and wanted to buy the hone. He stipulated that the would-be purchaser should pay for it by giving a banquet. They replied they were all willing to do this and asked him to hand it over to them. He threw the hone up into the air, however, and as they all wanted to catch it, it ended with them all cutting one another's throats with their scythes.

'Óðin sought lodgings for the night with Suttung's brother, a giant called Baugi. Baugi said that his affairs were in a bad way; he told him that nine of his serfs had been killed and said that he had no hope of finding any other labourers. Óðin, giving his name as Bölverk, offered to do the work of nine men for Baugi, and asked as wages one drink of Suttung's mead. Baugi told him that he had nothing to do with the mead, adding that Suttung was anxious to keep it under his sole control, but he professed himself willing to go along with Bölverk to try to get hold of it. That summer Bölverk did the work of nine men for Baugi, and when winter came he asked Baugi for his wages. Then they both went to Suttung. Baugi told his brother Suttung of his bargain with Bölverk, but Suttung flatly refused them a single drop of mead. Then Bölverk said to Baugi that they must try to get hold of the mead by some kind of trick. Baugi said that that was a good idea. Bölverk then brought out the auger called Rati and said that if the auger would pierce it, Baugi was to bore a hole through the mountain. He did so. When Baugi said that the mountain had been pierced through, Bölverk blew into the hole left by the auger but chips flew up into his face. He realized then that Baugi wanted to cheat him, and told him to bore right through. Baugi bored again, and when Bölverk blew into the hole for the second time the chips were blown [all the way] through. Then Bölverk changed himself into a serpent and crawled into the auger-hole. Baugi stabbed at him with the auger but missed him. Bölverk came to where Gunnlöð was, and slept with her for three nights, and then she promised him three drinks of the mead. At his first drink he drank up all that was in Óðrörir, at his second, Boðn, and at his third, Són — and then he had finished all the mead. Then he changed himself into an eagle and flew away at top-speed. When Suttung saw the eagle in flight, however, he also took on eagle shape and flew after him. Now when the Æsir saw where Óðin was flying, they put their crocks out in the courtyard, and when Óðin came inside Ásgarð he spat the mead into the crocks. It was such a close shave that Suttung did not catch him, however, that he let some fall, but no one bothered about that. Anyone who wanted could have it; we call it the poetasters' share. Óðin gave Suttung's

mead to the Æsir and those men who can compose poetry. So
we call poetry Óðin's catch, Óðin's discovery, his drink and his
gift, and the drink of the Æsir.'

Bragi told Ægir that Thór had once gone to the east to fight
trolls, when Óðin rode Sleipnir into Giantland and came to the
giant called Hrungnir. Hrungnir asked who the man was in the
golden helmet who was riding through the air and over the sea,
adding that he had a remarkably fine horse. Óðin replied that he
would wager his head its equal was not to be found in Giantland.
Hrungnir said that Sleipnir was a fine horse, but maintained that
he possessed one called Gold-mane that could step out much
better, and losing his temper he sprang on to his mount and
galloped after Óðin, intending to pay him out for his big talk.
Óðin galloped on so hard that he was on the other side of a hill
on the horizon in no time, but Hrungnir was in such a towering
rage that, before he knew where he was, he was inside the gate
of Ásgarð. When he arrived at the door of the hall, the Æsir
invited him in to drink with them. He went into the hall and
asked to be served with drink. The beakers Thór was accustomed
to drink from were brought to him and Hrungnir tossed off both.
When he was drunk, big words were not in short supply; he
declared that he would pick up Valhalla and carry it into Giantland, sink Ásgarð in the sea and kill all the gods except Freyja and
Sif whom he would carry off home with him. Then Freyja went
to pour out more ale for him and he declared he would drink up
all the Æsir had. When the Æsir were tired of his big talk,
however, they summoned Thór. At once Thór came into the
hall in a fury with his hammer raised aloft and asking on whose
authority sly devils of giants were drinking there, and under
whose safe-conduct Hrungnir was inside Valhalla, and why
Freyja was waiting on him, as if it were a banquet of the gods.
Hrungnir looking at Thór in no friendly manner answered that
Óðin had invited him to drink with him, and that he was there
under his safe-conduct. Thór declared that Hrungnir would be

sorry for this invitation before he left. Hrungnir said that it would not enhance Thór's reputation to kill him unarmed as he was, and that it would be a greater test of courage if he dared to fight him on the frontier at Grjótúnagarðar.[1] 'I've been a great fool', he added, 'to leave my shield and hone at home; if I had my weapons we should fight a duel now. On the other hand, I pronounce you dastard if you are intending to kill me unarmed.' No one had ever challenged Thór to a duel before, so he would not on any account fail to meet Hrungnir in single combat. Hrungnir went off on his way home galloping furiously until he reached Giantland. This expedition of his and the fact that he had arranged to meet Thór won him great fame amongst the giants. They felt that it mattered a good deal which of them should prove victorious; they could expect the worst from Thór if Hrungnir perished, for he was strongest of them.

Then the giants made a man of clay at Grjótúnagarðar. He was nine leagues high and three broad under his armpits and they could not get a heart large enough to fit him, until they took a mare's, and this was not steady in him when Thór arrived. Hrungnir's heart is famous. It was of hard stone and sharp-edged and three-cornered like the runic character known as 'Hrungnir's heart' which has since been made that way. His head, too, was of stone, also the broad, stout shield which he held before him while he was standing at Grjótúnagarðar waiting for Thór. As weapon of attack he had a hone poised on his shoulder and he looked an ugly customer. At his side stood the clay giant called Mist Calf, and it was terrified. It is said that it made water when it saw Thór.

Thór went to the duelling ground, and with him Thjálfi. Then Thjálfi ran forward to where Hrungnir was standing and told him: 'You're taking a risk the way you're standing, giant, with your shield in front of you; Thór has seen you. Put it down on the ground beneath you for he will come at you from below.'

1 Stone Fence House.

Hrungnir shoved his shield under his feet and stood on it, grasping the hone with both hands. At once he saw flashes of lightning and heard great claps of thunder; he was seeing Thór in his divine wrath. [The god] bore down on him at tremendous speed and brandishing his hammer hurled it at Hrungnir from a great distance. Hrungnir lifted up the hone in both hands and flung it against the hammer, and the hone colliding with it in mid-air was smashed to pieces. One part of it fell to the ground and all hone quarries have come from those fragments. The other pierced Thór's head so that he fell forward on the earth. The hammer Mjöllnir, however, struck Hrungnir in the middle of his head shivering his skull into small fragments, and he fell prone across Thór with one leg over Thór's neck. Thjálfi attacked Mist Calf and he fell with little renown.

Then Thjálfi went up to Thór to lift Hrungnir's leg off him, but he could not move it at all. When they heard that Thór was down, all the Æsir went up to him to lift off the leg, but they were unable to do anything. After that Magni, the son of Thór and Járnsaxa,[1] came up to them — he was three years old then — and he flung Hrungnir's leg off Thór saying: 'What a pity I didn't come sooner, father; I reckon I'd have struck the giant dead with my bare fist if I had met him.' Thór stood up then and gave his son a fine welcome saying he would be a strong man: 'And', said he, 'I'll give you the horse Gold-mane' — which Hrungnir had had. Óðin spoke then declaring that Thór was doing wrong to give a fine horse like that to the son of a giantess instead of to his own father.

Thór went home to Thrúðvangar with the hone stuck in his head. Then the sibyl called Gróa, wife of Aurvandil the Brave, came to him and recited spells over Thór until the hone worked loose. When Thór noticed that and felt that there was a chance of her getting it out, he wanted to reward Gróa for healing him and to make her happy. He told her the [good] news that he had

1 Iron Cutlass, a giantess.

waded south over Élivágar carrying Aurvandil on his back in a
basket out of Giantland in the north, and, in proof of this, that
one of his toes had stuck out of the basket and been frozen, so
Thór had broken it off and thrown it up into the sky and made
of it the star called Aurvandil's Toe. Thór added that it would
not be long before Aurvandil came home. Gróa was so delighted,
however, that she forgot her spells, and the hone did not work
any looser; it is still in Thór's head. Hones should never be
thrown across the floor as, in that case, the hone is moved that is
stuck in Thór's head.

Thjóðólf of Hvin has made up a poem about this story in
Haustlöng.[1]

Then Ægir said: 'I've been thinking that Hrungnir was a
powerful person. Did Thór perform any more great exploits
when he was fighting trolls?'

Then Bragi answered: 'The story of Thór's journey to
Geirröðargarðar is well worth the telling. On that occasion he had
neither the hammer Mjöllnir nor the belt of strength nor the iron
gauntlets, and Loki who went with him was to blame for that.
It had happened once to Loki, when he was flying about amusing
himself in Frigg's falcon coat, that out of curiosity he flew into
Geirröð's grounds. He saw there a great hall, and settled on a
window-ledge and looked in. Geirröð, however, caught sight of
him and ordered the bird to be captured and brought to him.
The messenger found it hard to climb up the wall of the hall; it
was so high. Loki was delighted that the man had such difficulty
in approaching him and had no intention of flying away, until
he had completed the tricky ascent. When the man reached out
for him, he spread his wings for flight, bracing his feet but found
them caught. Then Loki was seized and brought before giant
Geirröð and, when the giant saw his eyes, he suspected that they
were a man's and bade him answer him, but Loki kept silent.
Then Geirröð shut Loki up in a chest and starved him there for

1 Autumn long?

three months. When Geirröð took him out then and required him to speak, Loki told who he was and promised Geirröð on oath to bring Thór into Geirröð's stronghold without either hammer or belt of strength.

'Thór came to stay with a giantess called Gríð, the mother of Víðar the Silent. She told Thór the truth about giant Geirröð, that he was as cunning as a fox and a dangerous enemy. She lent him her belt of strength and iron gloves and her staff which is called Gríð's stick.

'Thór travelled until he reached the Vimur which is a very big river. He put on the belt of strength and braced himself against the current by leaning on Gríð's stick while Loki clung to the belt. When Thór reached midstream, the water rose so that it was breaking over his shoulders. Then Thór said this:

> Vimur, don't wax now
> I happen to be wading through
> you on my way to the giants;
> you know that if you do,
> so will my strength divine,
> until it reaches up as high as heaven!

Then Thór looked up a rocky ravine and saw Geirröð's daughter, Gjálp, standing there astride the river, and it was she who was causing it to swell. He picked up a great boulder from the river and flung it at her with the words: "A river must be dammed at its fountain-head!" He did not miss what he aimed at. At that moment he was carried ashore and catching hold of a rowan tree climbed in this way out of the river. This is why we say that the rowan is Thór's salvation.

'When Thór came to Geirröð, he and his companions were shown into a goat-shed for a lodging, with a single chair for a seat, on which Thór sat down. He then became aware that the chair was moving up to the roof with him. He thrust Gríð's stick against the roof, pushing himself down hard into the chair. There was a great crash accompanied by loud screaming.

Geirröð's two daughters, Gjálp and Greip, had been under the chair and he had broken both their backs. Then Geirröð had Thór called into the hall to compete with him in games of skill. There were huge fires down the whole length of the hall and, when Thór came face to face with Geirröð, Geirröð picked up a red-hot bolt of iron with a pair of tongs and threw it at him. Thór, however, caught it in mid-air with his iron gauntlets and Geirröð ran behind an iron pillar for safety. Thór threw the bolt and it went through the pillar and through Geirröð and through the wall and so outside and into the earth.'

'Why is gold called Sif's hair?'

'Once, for a joke, Loki, Laufey's son, cut off all Sif's hair, but when Thór got to know this he seized Loki and would have broken every bone in his body, had he not sworn to persuade the dark elves to make hair from gold for Sif that would grow like other hair. After that Loki went to the dwarfs called the sons of Ívaldi, and they made the hair and Skíðblaðnir and the spear that Óðin had, which is called Gungnir. Then Loki wagered his head with a dwarf called Brokk that his brother Eitri would not be able to make three other treasures as fine as these. When they came to the smithy, Eitri laid a pigskin in the furnace and told his brother Brokk to work the bellows and not to stop until he had taken what he had put there out of the forge. No sooner had he left the smithy than a fly settled on Brokk's hand and stung him, as he was working the bellows, but he kept them going as before, until the smith took the object from the forge — and there was a boar with bristles of gold.

'Next he put gold in the furnace and told him to blow without stopping until he returned. He went away, and then the fly came and settled on Brokk's neck, stinging him twice as badly as before. He went on blowing, however, until the smith took from the forge the gold ring called Draupnir.

'Then he put iron in the furnace and told him to blow, and said that everything would be spoiled if the bellows stopped working. This time the fly settled between his eyes and stung him on the eyelids so that the blood ran into his eyes and he could not see at all. He stopped the bellows and as quickly as possible brushed the fly away with one hand. At that moment the smith came in and said that everything in the furnace had been within an ace of being spoiled. Then he took from the forge a hammer and gave all the treasures to his brother Brokk, telling him to take them to Ásgarð to settle the wager.

'When he and Loki brought out their treasures, the Æsir sat down on their thrones and the verdict given by Óðin, Thór and Frey was to stand good. Loki then gave Óðin the spear, Gungnir; Thór, the hair Sif was to have; and Frey, Skíðblaðnir, and he explained what sort of treasures they were: the spear never missed its mark, the hair would grow to her skin as soon as it was put on Sif's head, and Skíðblaðnir got a breeze to take it where it had to go as soon as its sail was hoisted, and it could be folded together like a cloth and carried in one's pouch, if so desired. Then Brokk produced his treasures. He gave Óðin the ring, saying that every ninth night eight others as heavy as itself would drop from it. To Frey he gave the boar, saying that it could run through the air and over the sea day or night faster than any horse, and that no matter how gloomy it might be at night or in the world of darkness, it would always be brilliantly light where it was travelling; its bristles shone so. Then he gave the hammer to Thór and said that he could hit anything that was in his way with it as hard as he could and the hammer would never break; and if he hurled it at anything he would never lose it — no matter how far it was flung it would return to his hand; also, if he desired, it could become so small that he could keep it in his shirt. It had, however, one fault; it was rather short in the handle.

'The decision of the gods was that the hammer was the most valuable of all the treasures and the best defence against the frost ogres, and they decided that the dwarf had won the wager. Then Loki offered to redeem his head but the dwarf said that he could not expect to do that. "Catch me, then!" said Loki, and when the dwarf tried to seize him he was already a long way off. Loki had shoes in which he could run through the air and over the sea. Then the dwarf asked Thór to catch him and he did so. The dwarf wanted to cut off his head, but Loki said he had a claim on his head but not his neck. The dwarf took a thong and a knife and tried to pierce holes in Loki's lips to sew them up, but the knife would not cut. Then he said that his brother's awl would be better and, as soon as he had mentioned it, there it was, and it pierced the lips. He sewed up the mouth, and [Loki] tore the thong out through the holes. The thong with which Loki's mouth was sewn up is called Vartari.'

'What is the reason for calling gold "otter's ransom"?'

'It is said that when the Æsir, Óðin and Loki and Hœnir were exploring the whole world, they came to a river and went along it to a waterfall, and by the waterfall was an otter which was eating a salmon it had caught there and it was half-asleep. Loki picked up a stone and flung it at the otter, striking it on the head. Then Loki boasted of his catch — with one throw he had bagged an otter and a salmon. They took the salmon and the otter away with them and came to a farm which they entered. The farmer living there was called Hreiðmar. He was a powerful man with much skill in magic. The Æsir asked the farmer for lodgings there for the night, saying that they had plenty of food, and they showed him their catch. When Hreiðmar saw the otter, however, he called his sons Fáfnir and Regin, and told them that their brother, Otter, had been killed, and also who had done the deed. Then father and sons attacked the Æsir and made them prisoner and bound them, telling them that the otter was Hreiðmar's son. The Æsir offered to pay as large a ransom as Hreiðmar himself should demand, and those terms were agreed on and confirmed by oath. Then the otter was flayed, and Hreiðmar took the skin and told them that they had to fill it and completely cover it into the bargain with red gold. That would reconcile them. Óðin then sent Loki to the World-of-dark-elves, and he came to the dwarf called Andvari. He was in a pool in his fish shape, and Loki seizing him exacted as ransom all the gold he had in his rock dwelling. When they got there the dwarf produced all the gold he possessed and it was a very great sum of money, but he kept back in his hand a little gold ring. Loki noticed this and told him to give him the ring. The dwarf begged him not to take it from him, saying that if only he were allowed to keep it he could by its means become wealthy again. Loki said that he was to be left without a single penny and taking the ring from him was going away, when the dwarf declared that the ring would destroy everyone who owned it. Loki replied that that was all to the good, adding that the prophecy should be fulfilled, provided that he himself pronounced it in the ears of those about to take over the ring.

'He went away and came to Hreiðmar and showed the gold ring to Óðin. When Óðin saw it he admired it for its beauty and kept it back, although he paid the gold to Hreiðmar. Hreiðmar stuffed the skin to bursting and when it was full raised it up on end. Then Óðin went up to it to cover it with gold and, this done, he asked Hreiðmar to look and see if the skin was not completely hidden. Hreiðmar took a good look at it and caught sight of one whisker. He ordered this to be concealed or otherwise, he said, their agreement would be at an end. Then Óðin drew the ring from his finger and concealed the whisker, saying that now they had paid the otter's ransom. When, however, Óðin had taken his spear and Loki his shoes and there was no reason they should be afraid, Loki declared that what Andvari had said should hold good, that that ring and that gold would destroy whosoever owned them. That has been the case ever since. Now you know why gold is called otter's ransom or the forced payment of the Æsir or metal-of-strife.'

'Is anything more known about this gold?'

'Hreiðmar accepted the gold as ransom for his son, and Fáfnir and Regin asked for some of it as a ransom for their brother. Hreiðmar did not give them a single penny of it. The brothers were wicked enough to kill their father for the gold. Then Regin asked Fáfnir to go shares in the gold, but Fáfnir replied that there was little likelihood that he would share with his brother the gold for which he had killed his father, and he told Regin to go away or else he would meet with Hreiðmar's fate. Fáfnir had taken a helmet which had been Hreiðmar's and was wearing it; this struck fear into all beholders and was called the helmet of terror. He also had the sword known as Hrotti. Regin owned a sword called Refil. He took to flight but Fáfnir went up on to Gnita Heath and, making a lair there, turned himself into a dragon and lay down on the gold.

'Then Regin went to King Hjálprek in Tý[1] and became his smith there. He adopted as his foster son Sigurð, son of Sigmund, son of Völsung and Hjördis, Eylimi's daughter. On account of his family, strength and courage, Sigurð was the most famous of all warrior kings. Regin told him where Fáfnir was lying on the gold and egged him on to seek the treasure. Regin made the sword called Gram. This was so sharp that, when Sigurð thrust it into running water, he cut in two a lock of wool carried against the blade by the current. With the same sword Sigurð clove Regin's anvil to the stock. After that Sigurð and Regin went to Gnita Heath and Sigurð dug pits in Fáfnir's path and sat down in one. When Fáfnir, crawling on his way down to the water, came over the pit, Sigurð ran him through with his sword and that was his death. Then Regin came and said that Sigurð had killed his brother, and offered him terms on condition that he took Fáfnir's heart and roasted it over a fire. Regin himself lay down and drank Fáfnir's blood and then went to sleep. When Sigurð thought the heart he was roasting was done, he touched it with his finger to see how tender it was, and the juice from it ran on to his finger, burning it, so he put this into his mouth. When

1 In Jutland.

the blood came on to his tongue, however, he understood the language of birds and knew what the nuthatches sitting in the branches were saying. One said:

> There sits Sigurð
> blood-bespattered,
> Fáfnir's heart
> roasts at the fire;
> wise that liberal prince
> would appear to me
> should he eat
> that shining heart.

> There lies Regin, said another,
> revolving in his mind
> how to betray
> the lad who trusts him;
> in wrath he is collecting
> crooked words together,
> he longs contriver-of-evil
> to avenge his brother.

Then Sigurð went up to Regin and killed him, and afterwards to his horse which was called Grani and rode until he came to Fáfnir's lair. There he took the gold and making it into packs put it on Grani's back, mounted himself and rode on his way.

'Now you know the story explaining why gold is called Fáfnir's abode or lair, or the metal of Gnita Heath, or Grani's burden.

'Sigurð rode on then until he came to a hall on a mountain. In it was sleeping a woman in helmet and coat of mail. He drew his sword and cut the mail-coat from her. Then she woke up and said she was called Hild. Her name was Brynhild and she was a valkyrie. Sigurð rode away from there and came to a king called Gjúki. His wife was called Grímhild and their children were Gunnar, Högni, Guðrún and Guðný. Gotthorm was Gjúki's stepson. Sigurð stayed there for a long time and married Guðrún, Gjúki's daughter, and Gunnar and Högni became sworn brothers

of Sigurð's. Soon after Sigurð and the sons of Gjúki went to ask
Atli Buðlason for his sister, Brynhild, as Gunnar's wife. She lived
at Hindafjall and there was a rampart of flame round her hall.
She had vowed only to marry that man who dared ride through
the flames. Sigurð and the Gjúkungar — they are also called the
Niflungar[1] — rode up on to the mountain and Gunnar was to
ride through the rampart of flame. He had a horse called Goti but
it did not dare leap into the fire. Sigurð and Gunnar then changed
shapes and also names, because Grani would not move under any
man but Sigurð, and Sigurð vaulting on to Grani rode the
rampart of flame. That evening he married Brynhild but, when
they went to bed, he drew the sword Gram from its sheath and
laid it between them. In the morning when he got up and
dressed, however, he gave Brynhild as a wedding present the
gold ring Loki had taken from Andvari, receiving another from
her in exchange. Then Sigurð jumped on to his horse and rode
back to his companions. He and Gunnar changed shapes again
and went back to Gjúki with Brynhild. Sigurð had two children
by Guðrún, Sigmund and Svanhild.

'On one occasion Brynhild and Guðrún went down to the
water to wash their hair. When they reached the river, Brynhild
waded out further from the bank, saying that she was not going
to use the water in which Guðrún had rinsed her hair for her own
head, since she had the more valiant husband. Guðrún went into
the river after her then, and said that she had a right to wash her
hair in water higher up the river, since she had a husband whom
neither Gunnar nor anyone else in the world could match in
courage, because he had killed Fáfnir and Regin and had inherited
the property of both. Then Brynhild answered: "Sigurð did not
dare ride the rampart of flame: Gunnar did — that counts for
more." Guðrún laughed then and said: "You think it was
Gunnar who rode the flames? The man you slept with was the
one who gave me this gold ring, and the ring you are wearing

1 Nibelungs.

and which you received as a wedding gift is called Andvari's treasure, and I don't think that Gunnar got it on Gnita Heath." At that Brynhild was silent and went home.

'Afterwards she urged Gunnar and Högni to kill Sigurð but, because they were his sworn brothers, they persuaded their brother Gotthorm to kill him. He ran Sigurð through with a sword while he was sleeping, but, when Sigurð felt the wound, he hurled the sword after Gotthorm so that it cut him asunder through the middle. Sigurð and his three-year-old son called Sigmund, whom they also killed, perished there. After that Brynhild fell on her sword and she was burned with Sigurð. Gunnar and Högni, however, took Fáfnir's inheritance then and Andvari's treasure and ruled the country.

'Brynhild's brother, Atli Buðlason, married Guðrún, once the wife of Sigurð, and they had children together. King Atli invited Gunnar and Högni to stay with him and they went on this visit. Before leaving home, however, they hid the gold that was Fáfnir's inheritance in the Rhine, and it has never been found since. King Atli had troops to oppose them and these fought Gunnar and Högni and took them prisoner. King Atli had Högni's heart cut out of him while he was still living and that was his death. He had Gunnar flung into a snake-pit. A harp was procured for him in secret and, because his hands were tied, he played it with his toes in such a way that all the snakes went to sleep, but for one adder, which made for him and gnawing its way through the cartilage of his breast-bone thrust its head through the hole and buried its fangs in his liver until he was dead. Gunnar and Högni are called Niflungar or Gjúkungar; for this reason gold is called the treasure or inheritance of the Niflungar.

'A little later Guðrún killed her two sons and had goblets decorated with silver and gold made from their skulls. Then the funeral feast of the Niflungar was celebrated. From these goblets Guðrún had King Atli served with mead which was mixed with the boys' blood, and she had their hearts roasted and given the king to eat at the same banquet. When this had been done she told him about it in many ugly words. There was no lack of intoxicating mead there so that most people fell asleep where they were sitting. That same night she went to the king when he was asleep, and with her Högni's son, and they made an armed attack on him and that was his death. Then they set fire to the hall and burned the people inside it.

'After that she went down to the sea and ran into it to drown herself. She was drifted over the fiord, however, and came ashore in King Jónak's country, and when he saw her he took her home and married her. They had three sons with these names: Sörli, Hamðir, and Erp. These had hair as black as the raven, like Gunnar and Högni and the other Niflungar. Sigurð's daughter, Svanhild, grew up there and she was a very lovely woman. King Jörmunrekk the Mighty heard of this and sent his son Randvér to ask her hand in marriage for him. When he came to Jónak, Svanhild was given into his custody and he was to take her to Jörmunrekk. Then Bikki said that it would be more suitable for Randvér to marry Svanhild, since he was young, indeed they both were, whereas Jörmunrekk was an old man. The young people were delighted with this plan. Soon after Bikki told the king and Jörmunrekk had his son seized and led to the gallows. Randvér took his hawk then, and plucking off its feathers, ordered it to be sent to his father. After that he was hanged. When King Jörmunrekk saw the hawk, it struck him that just as the hawk stripped of its feathers was unable to fly, so, now that he was an old man and without a son, had he crippled his kingdom. Once when he was riding home from a wood in which he and his court had been hunting, King Jörmunrekk caught sight of Svanhild where she sat drying her hair. They rode her down and trampled her to death under their horses' hoofs.

'When Guðrún heard this, she egged on her sons to avenge Svanhild and, when they were making ready for the expedition, procured for them coats of mail and helmets which were so strong that no weapon could pierce them. She advised them, when they reached King Jörmunrekk, to attack him at night in his sleep. Sörli and Hamðir were to cut off his hands and feet, and Erp his head. On the way, however, they asked Erp to what extent they could rely on him when they came to grips with Jörmunrekk. He replied that he would help them as the hand does the foot. They said that the hand gave no help at all to the foot and they were so annoyed with their mother for having sent them out with taunts that they wanted to do what would hurt her most, so they killed Erp because she loved him best. A little later, one of Sörli's feet slipped as he was walking, and he supported himself with his hand. Then he said: "Hand helped foot just now. It would be better if Erp was alive."

'They came to King Jörmunrekk one night when he was asleep, and were cutting off his hands and feet when he awoke and shouted to his men to rouse themselves. Hamðir said: "His head would be off now, if Erp were alive!" Then Jörmunrekk's bodyguard got up and attacked them, but they could not overcome them with weapons, so Jörmunrekk called out to them to use stones. This was done, and Sörli and Hamðir fell there. With them the whole Gjúkung line came to an end.

'Sigurd left a daughter called Áslaug who was fostered by Heimir in Hlymdalir and great families have come from her.

'It is said that Sigmund Völsungsson was so strong that he could drink poison without coming to harm, and that Sinfjötli, his son, and Sigurð had such hard skins that their naked bodies were immune to poison.'

'Why is gold called Fróði's flour?'

'There is a story about this to the effect that there was a son of Óðin's called Skjöld from whom the Skjöldungar have come. He ruled the country which is now called Denmark (and at that time, Gotland) and had a palace there. Skjöld had a son called Friðleif who ruled the country after him. Friðleif's son was called Fróði. He inherited the kingdom after his father at the time when the

Emperor Augustus made peace over the whole world. Christ was born then. However, because Fróði was the most powerful of all the Scandinavian kings, all the northern nations ascribe that peace to him, and the Norsemen call it the Peace of Fróði. No man injured another, even although he was confronted with the slayer of his father or brother, free or in bonds. Neither were there any thieves or robbers, so that a gold ring lay untouched for a long time on the Heath of Jelling.[1] King Fróði was invited to stay with the king Fjölnir of Sweden. There he bought two women slaves, who were big and strong, called Fenja and Menja. In Denmark at that time there were two millstones so huge that no one had sufficient strength to turn them. These millstones were the sort that ground whatever the miller required. The mill was called Grotti and the name of the man who gave it to King Fróði was Hangjaw. King Fróði had the slaves taken to the mill and he told them to grind Fróði's gold and peace and prosperity. He would not allow them to rest or sleep for longer than the cuckoo stops its calling or it takes to ask people for a hearing. They are said then to have composed the song known as *Grotti's Song* and, before they finished it, they ground out an army against King Fróði, so that that same night a viking called Mýsing came and killed Fróði and captured a great deal of spoil. With that the Peace of Fróði came to an end.

'Mýsing took Grotti and Fenja and Menja away with him and ordered them to grind salt. At midnight they asked him if he was not tired of salt, but he told them to go on grinding. They had ground on for a short time only when the ship sank, and where the sea poured into the eye of the hand-mill was a whirlpool there afterwards in the ocean. It was then that the sea became salt.'

'Why is gold called Kraki's seed?'

'There was a king in Denmark called Hrólf Kraki. On account of his mildness, valour and modesty he was in the first rank of ancient kings. Here is an example of his modesty which is often

1 In Jutland.

quoted in ancient tales. A small boy, and a poor one at that, called Vögg, came into Hrólf's palace when the king was young in years and slight of build. Vögg came into his presence and looked him up and down. Then the king asked: "What are you wanting to take the measure of, lad, looking at me like this?" Vögg replied: "When I was at home, I heard people say that King Hrólf of Hleiðr[1] was the greatest king in Scandinavia, and now there's a lanky little bit of a fellow sitting on the throne and you call him king!" The king answered: "You have given me a name, lad; I'm to be called Kraki, and it's usual for a 'name-fastening' to be accompanied by a present. Now, I can't see that you've got any such present to give me that I'd like, so the one who has is going to give." Taking a gold ring from his finger he gave it to the boy. Then Vögg said: "Blessing on you for your gift, king, and I promise you that I will kill the man who kills you." The king laughed at that and said: "Vögg is contented with little."

'Here follows an example of Hrólf's valour. There was a king ruling Uppsala called Aðils who married Hrólf Kraki's mother, Yrsa. He was at war with a king of Norway called Áli, and they fought a great battle on Lake Vener. King Aðils sent a message to Hrólf Kraki to come to his assistance, promising to pay every man in his army while they were campaigning, and the king himself was to choose for his own three treasures from Sweden. King Hrólf was unable to go on account of his war with the Saxons, but he sent Aðils his twelve berserks. Böðvar Bjarki was one: [amongst the others were] Hjalti the Valiant, Hvítserk the Bold, Vött, Véseti, the brothers Svipdag and Beiguð. In that battle King Áli and most of his troops fell, and King Aðils despoiled him of his helmet Battle-pig and his horse Raven. Hrólf's twelve berserks asked for their pay, three pounds of gold each, and they also asked for the treasures they were choosing for King Hrólf so that they could take them to him, namely, the

1 Leire.

helmet Battle-pig, the coat of mail known as Finn's legacy, which could not be pierced by any weapon, and the gold ring called Svíagríss, which had been in the possession of Aðils' ancestors. The king, however, refused them all these treasures and kept back their pay into the bargain. The berserks went away very disgruntled and informed King Hrólf of the situation. He set out for Uppsala at once; and when he had sailed his ships up the river Fyris, he made for Uppsala on horseback and with him his twelve berserks, all of them without safe-conduct. His mother Yrsa welcomed him and accompanied him to his quarters, but not to the king's palace. Great fires were made for them and they were given ale to drink. Then King Aðils' men came and threw logs on to the fires and they became so big that Hrólf Kraki and his men had their clothes burned off them, and Aðils' men asked: "Is it true that Hrólf Kraki and his berserks flee neither fire nor sword?" At that Hrólf Kraki and all of them jumped up, and he said: "Let's make the fires at Aðils' still larger", and taking his shield he flung it on to the fire and jumped over it while it was still burning. He added: "The man who jumps over a fire isn't running away from it." One after another his men followed suit, and then they seized those who had made the fires larger and flung them into them. After that Yrsa came and gave Hrólf Kraki a horn full of gold and along with it the ring Svíagríss, and bade him ride away for reinforcements. They leaped on to their horses and rode down on to the Plains of Fyris. Then they saw that King Aðils with a fully equipped army was riding after them with the intention of destroying them. King Hrólf Kraki took the gold out of the horn with his right hand and strewed it all along the way. When the Swedes saw that, they jumped down from their saddles and each took what he could grab. King Aðils, however, ordered them to ride on and went on riding himself at a gallop. His horse was called Slungnir and it was a very swift one. When King Hrólf Kraki saw that King Aðils was gaining on him, he took the ring Svíagríss and flinging it at him bade him accept it as a gift. King Aðils rode at the ring, picked it up with his spear-point and let it slip down to the socket. King Hrólf Kraki turned round then, saw him stooping down and said: "I've made the mightiest of the Swedes grovel like a pig", and with that they parted.

'For this reason gold is called the seed of Kraki or of the Plains of Fyris.

'Battle is called the gale or tempest, and weapons the fires or staves of the Hjaðningar, and here's the story about that.

'There was a king called Högni who had a daughter whose name was Hild. A king called Heðin Hjarrandason made her a prisoner of war whilst Högni was away at a royal assembly. When, however, he heard that his kingdom had been raided and his daughter carried off, he went to look for Heðin with his army. He heard that he had sailed to the north. When Högni came to Norway, however, he heard that Heðin had sailed for the British Isles. Then Högni sailed after him all the way to Orkney, and when he arrived at the island called Hoy, there in front of him was Heðin with his army. Hild went to meet her father and offered him a necklace from Heðin in reconciliation. She also let him understand, however, that Heðin was ready to fight and that Högni could not hope for any mercy from him. Högni answered his daughter curtly and, when she came to Heðin, she told him that Högni had refused to come to terms and bade him prepare for battle. So both of them went up on to the island and drew up their forces. Then Heðin called out to his father-in-law, Högni, offering him terms and a great deal of gold as compensation. Högni answered: "You are too late in making this offer for terms; I've drawn Dáin's heirloom which was made by the dwarfs; every time it is bared it slays its man, it never misses a stroke and no one recovers from the wound it gives." Heðin said: "You're boasting only of a sword, not of victory. I call any sword good that serves its master well."

'They began the battle called the Battle of the Hjaðningar and they fought all day long. In the evening the kings went on board their ships. Hild, however, went to the battlefield by night and aroused all the dead by witchcraft. The kings went on to the battlefield a second day and fought, and with them all those who had fallen on the previous day. Day after day the battle went on, in such a way that all who fell and all weapons [left] lying on the battlefield, and even the shields too, turned to stone. At dawn, however, all the dead men got up and fought and all their weapons became new. So it says in the poems that the Battle of the Hjaðningar will last until the Twilight of the Gods. The poet Bragi composed a poem on this story in the *Lay of Ragnar Shaggy-Breeks.*'

INDEX

Index

Index

Index

Index

Index

Index

Index

Index